praise for
The Tarot Apothecary

I've been using Ailynn's potions for years. They ground me when I'm overcome with energy, and they raise my inner fire when I have to teach. And I'm excited for her to share all her secrets inside *The Tarot Apothecary*. Now you can blend and craft unique potions to transform your life.

—Jaymi Elford, author
of *Tarot Inspired Life*

THE
TAROT
Apothecary

About the Author

Ailynn E. Halvorson is a deep believer in the mysteries that surround us. As a child she always wanted to grow up to be a witch or a gypsy fortuneteller. At the age of ten, her older sister introduced her to the tarot, and the cards have been a part of her life ever since. Today she still dwells in the magic of the world. Ailynn is a certified clinical aromatherapist who works with essential oils to call in the spirit of the oils and assist in clarity for the individual. Ailynn has been teaching and reading tarot professionally for more than twelve years. Ailynn's soul purpose is to lead others on their path to success and happiness through the use of the plant kingdom and the magic and power of tarot. Please visit her website at www.byailynn.com.

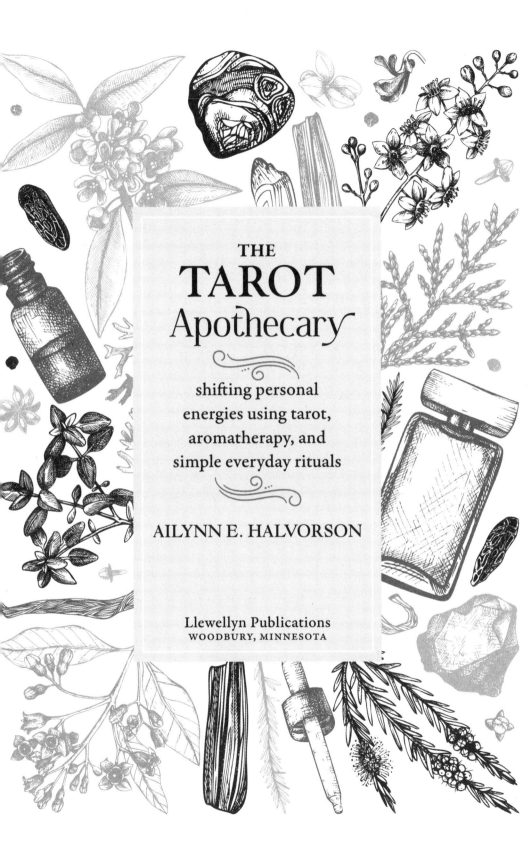

THE
TAROT
Apothecary

shifting personal
energies using tarot,
aromatherapy, and
simple everyday rituals

AILYNN E. HALVORSON

Llewellyn Publications
WOODBURY, MINNESOTA

FIRST EDITION
First Printing, 2022

Book design by Rebecca Zins
Cover design by Shannon McKuhen

Llewellyn is a registered trademark of Llewellyn Worldwide Ltd.

Library of Congress Cataloging-In-Publication Data
Pending
ISBN 978-0-7387-7133-5

Llewellyn Publications
A Division of Llewellyn Worldwide Ltd.
2143 Wooddale Drive
Woodbury, MN 55125-2989

www.llewellyn.com
Printed in the United States of America

In memory of my sister Barbara Ann Shepherd, who brought home the first tarot deck that I had the privilege to hold in my hands. My sister taught and grounded me in the magic of the tarot. I am forever grateful to her, and she will always be a guide in my life.

Acknowledgments

Special thanks to my husband, Leif, for his grounding support. He has always loved me for who I am and supported my magic. What a powerful guide he is in my life.

Thanks to my beautiful daughter, Emily Rose, who is such a magical soul. Emily shares herself bravely with this world and has followed my footsteps into the world of tarot and magic. What a blessing she has been in my life.

Thanks to Jaymi Elford for her guiding hand and for teaching me the power of the word.

Thanks to Hilary Parry Haggerty for her support and knowledge.

Thanks to Shanti Dechen, CCAP, CAI, LMT, for teaching me the power of aromatherapy.

Most special thanks to the tarot community, whose support, knowledge, and integrity have been more than an inspiration to me. Thanks for leading the way.

Contents

Part Two
Pulling It All Together

Part Three
What's Next?

Introduction

The tarot apothecary approach teaches you the skills to honor your own magic. Here you'll learn how to:

- spend time with your chosen tarot archetype in imaginative meditation
- calculate your personal tarot numerology
- blend essential oils
- work with stones
- write mantras to work with your magical potion
- create magical teas

While I teach you the basics, you'll use your personality, power, and creativity to decide how you want to work with a chosen energy and how you wish to step forward on your path. While we are not always in control of what happens in life, we do have the power to determine how we will walk through life, as well as how we learn from our experiences. Embrace your personal magic, your personal power, and reach your desired destination standing strong and centered in your belief in yourself as this book guides you. Our mother, the earth, has gifted us with her powerful gifts and messages from the plant kingdom. We need to be open to believe and receive.

Let the journey begin.

Part One

Discovering Self
and the Energies
that Surround You

1

The Tarot Apothecary Approach

The Tarot Apothecary lays out a magical approach to the tarot that calls in the five wisdoms of tarot, aromatherapy, numerology, imaginative journey (the state of allowing your mind and imagination to journey outside of yourself with a predetermined intention), and simple everyday ritual. This creates a container of magical energies that allows for desired shifts in personal energy. This approach allows you to create your own personal cauldron of magic for movement forward.

This book is designed to be a companion to your personal tarot deck. As we travel through life and through the energies of the cards, it is important to learn how to work with and walk through the energy of each card. This allows you to experience and learn from the card's message. Sometimes an energy needs to be embraced and worked with; other times we need to release the overbearing and difficult energy so we can walk through to the other side. In these circumstances you can ask for support through embracing the energy of a chosen tarot card and working with plant allies to assist on the journey.

The tarot apothecary approach uses the twenty-two major arcana cards and the four queens within the tarot. In chapter 2 we will discover the power that each major arcana card carries and how they can assist you on your journey. Listed below is just a small portion of what you will discover about each card. This information will help you to choose the archetype that best suits you for movement forward on your desired path:

- the energy of the card
- plant allies and their energy to assist on the journey
- which queens can be of assistance to you as you work through the major arcana's energy
- companion cards

This approach is designed to bring support, courage, and confidence to move through a current energy, allowing you to embrace and learn the card's message. This approach also allows you to call in any energy you may require to create and step forward on your personal path. As we work with plant allies, stones, colors, meditative journeys, and mantras, we gain control in our life and allow ourselves to grow.

This book is written from personal experience, as well as my path of assisting tarot and aromatherapy clients, friends, and family on their adventures through the cards. When I first started working with tarot, I did not try to embrace the energy of the cards I worked with. I believed the influence of the card would come into my life and I would have to either endure or enjoy the energy, depending on the card. I never would have thought of walking through and learning from the message of the card, but this new way of embracing each card came to me as I began my journey of working with essential oils and plant allies. I found that if I embraced the energy of the card and called in support from the plant kingdom, I was able to transition through the energy. I felt supported and grounded. As I started to embrace this new way of thinking, allowing myself to feel the energy of the card, at times I found the message of the card was too much and I was either frightened or too anxious to allow for total submergence into my personal journey. This is when I discovered that one can ask for support.

Shifting personal energies by calling in a chosen energy can give you more options and control in life. In working with tarot, we can call in support not only from the twenty-two major arcana cards and the four queens; we also have the four elements available to us. The suit of pentacles (earth element) brings in support, structure, grounding, abundance, nourishment, and trust in one's self. Cups (water element) support flow and open heart energy—the ability to be open to receive like the opening in a cup—as well as intuition, spirituality, compassion, and love. Water can support the beginning of movement forward and start a small flow. Wands (fire element) is movement outward, action, the spark, creativity, strength, courage, transformation, and leadership—energy at its highest. Swords (air element) support truth, communication, inspiration, clarity, and the ability to get things done, as well as focused intention. Calling in an element that is absent in a reading or that will support your intended goal helps immensely.

For example, when I was getting ready to teach my very first tarot class, I was terrified. I was talking myself out of teaching by listening to the voice in my head, my ego. *You are not worthy of teaching. What makes you think you have the knowledge to teach? Just cancel the class.* All of these thoughts raced through my mind. I pulled my cards out and read for myself. I needed to see what they had to say. I asked, "What is holding me back from teaching?" and received the Nine of Swords. I call this card "the Nightmare" because it is an air element card, which makes me ask, "What is going on in my mind?" The Nine of Swords shows fear, anxiety, and sleepless energy. "Fearful to move forward" was my answer. At that point, I decided I was too much in my head and not grounded in my body. By not standing strong, I was fearful.

I decided I did have something to say about tarot and if I did not start teaching now, I would lose the nerve and never teach. Since I felt the need to get back into my body and ground myself, I decided to work with essential oils. I wanted an earthy scent that would pull me back into my body with less emphasis on the mind. Scent is a very powerful ally. Scent can reform your thought process and create new memories. Is there a scent that takes you back to your childhood? Why not empower an essential oil or a blend with an intention that would create a shift in your being in the present day? By setting an intention behind a scent or blend of essential oils, you are creating a powerful new foundation for change of thoughts and therefore of mind. Essential oils also have the ability to pass through the blood–brain barrier and literally reach our blood stream and change the chemistry in our body. This all happens through breath and a simple inhalation of the oil. By working with essential oils and creating my own blend, I was setting an intention for a scent creation that would shift the energy in my mind and body to a less fearful and more grounded state.

My Queen of Pentacles spray was born that day. I went into the kitchen, pulled out every earthy oil I could find, and started blending. I paid no attention to what I was really doing. I wasn't trained at the time. I just mixed patchouli, vetiver, cypress, Virginia cedarwood, and clary sage. I added sweet orange essential oil for a drop of fire. The fire element helped set the intention of starting the spark within and supporting the energies of courage, confidence, and charisma. I turned all this into a spray that I used on my skin as a perfume and in the air to call the energy of the Queen of Pentacles into my external space, and I loved it. I wrote a mantra for myself and worked with the spray at least three times a day, spritzing the spray while repeating the mantra. Needless to say, I taught the class, and it was the first of many to come.

After creating my Queen of Pentacles spray, I started working one on one with the queens. I created a spray for each queen and sat in meditation with each queen individually. Each queen spoke with me, and I learned to honor and work within their individual energies. I designed and taught a class called Goddess Save the Queens: Embracing the Elemental Energies of the Four Queens within the Tarot. Herein I discovered the power of the queens. The tarot queens not only embrace the energy of the element they are a part of, but they *own* that energy, they *ooze* that energy. I learned through embracing the energy of a queen, you can *become* that queen. You embody her energy, be it earth, water, fire, or air. Through embracing a queen's energy, you have power, structure, and support based on each queen's elemental correspondence. You have the power you require to walk through your current journey. Even though you have embodied the queen's elemental energy, you are stepping out on your path as you.

Companion Cards

You can also ask the assistance of a companion card for support on the journey. In this approach, the companion card is based on numerology, which we'll cover in chapter 3. Let's say you are currently working with the energy of the Tower card. The Tower can be a difficult energy to walk through. However, the Tower is an important energy to learn from so you don't have to repeat this lesson again. In tarot the Tower card is fire energy; in order to create new ground for new growth, it burns up anything that needs to go.

This card can often be painful. Things fall away, sometimes unexpectedly. Life can change in an instant, and often the ego feels the brunt of the lightning strike. The question with this card is, do you want to embrace the burn? If so, call in more fire and burn that stuff up. If the energy is overwhelming and too hot for comfort, then call in the Queen of Pentacles to add a firm foundation to stand upon. She can create a container for the burn so it does not get out of control, and she can also allow support of self. One could call in the Queen of Cups for emotional support and trust in one's own intuition and internal knowing. You could also call in the energy of the companion card. The Tower is number 16 in the tarot. By reducing this number down to 7 $(1 + 6 = 7)$, we find the power of the Chariot, numbered seven in the major arcana.

The Chariot is water element energy, allowing the fire to cool a bit. The Chariot also reminds you to stay focused on your chosen direction. Don't allow your emotions to get in the way. These two aspects give you the ability to move through the fire. Do not react; just feel and continue on. Are you seeing how this works?

The next step is to summon the energy into our life. How do we embrace the energy of a card or call in support from another archetypal energy in the tarot? You can do this by embracing the energy of the support card and calling in plant allies to lead the way. Here we learn to embrace energies through the support of essential oils, herbs, and teas.

How do we determine which cards are influential in our life right now? There are many different ways to discover this. Often there is one card that sticks out during a tarot reading. Maybe the Hermit shows up, and you know that it is time to seek within for your answers. Embracing the Hermit would be your answer. The Hermit is earth element, so using essential oils that are grounding and earthy would be supportive.

I often work with what year I am in the tarot based on my numerology for the year. You will learn how to calculate your own personal numerology in chapter 3. I am currently in my Lovers year, so working with the Lovers and plant allies that support the energy of the Lovers are my go-to. The Lovers year embraces new relationships and allows for the release of some relationships. The Lovers year is about choice; one is often at a crossroads with this card. The Lovers is air element energy, so I work with plants such as lavender and peppermint, which also carry the energy of air. I also called in a second card, or archetypal energy, to support my Lovers year. In this case I chose the Fool as my second energy to work with. There was no calculation other than letting my intuition and mind select the card. I wanted to take a leap of faith into a career of writing. This was my crossroads: was I to stay in a "real" full-time job or could I find the courage to jump into a new life of writing? The Fool allows me to jump when needed.

You can also just decide to work with a certain card based on the energy you need at any time in your life, as I did with the Fool. I often call in a queen to help me embrace an elemental energy or the Magician for manifesting. All you have to do is look through the pack of cards and grab the image or the card that has the meaning you want to use. Then you can create an altar and call in the associated plant allies to guide you. An altar is a special space set aside for beauty, devotion, ritual, and focus on a specific energy, deity, or archetype. This helps to create a relationship with the energies you are currently working with.

At other times, we may not pull cards or read cards at all. Often we know what energy we are lacking or searching for. At these times, we can choose which queen or major arcana card we wish to work with. I search through my deck and pull my desired card from my spirit deck. A spirit deck is a special deck of only major arcana cards that I use for ritual. I often like to use specific decks for specific tasks. I use this deck for ritual and magical intentions only. I also have a special deck in which I really love the imagery of the queens, and this deck is my queens deck. I have often bought greeting cards with an especially beautiful feminine energy and elemental twist to them to use as images of the queens on my altars. Working with one deck or one set of images allows for a stationary, familiar image for your ritual work with the major arcana and queen workings. Please remember that the only deck that is needed for the tarot apothecary approach is your own personal deck. There are many tarot decks out in the world, and the only deck that is required is the one you personally have chosen to work with.

Let's say we wish to work with the energy of the Magician. Here we can work with the earth element (for manifesting upon the earth). Since the Magician also includes the four elements upon his table, we can choose to call in a second elemental energy. What do you wish to manifest upon the earth? Is it a structure, abundance, fertility? These are earth elemental energies. Are you writing, speaking, or singing? Do you need to be truthful with yourself to move forward? Ask the air element to help. The fire element calls in courage and charisma. Use fire to support your creative project, magic, or transformation. Ask the water element for emotional support, healing a blocked energy, or compassion for self. In this manner *we* are the Magician and can manifest our desires.

You don't have to work with an elemental energy for a long time. Sometimes you can call in a particular elemental energy for an hour or a day. Maybe I have a job interview; in this case, I would call in a queen or major arcana card to encompass the elemental flow needed. Maybe the earth element in its Queen of Pentacles form can help me be internally grounded and self-sufficient. Maybe fire, the Queen of Wands, for leadership, charisma, and courage; water, the

Queen of Cups, for compassion and caring energy; or air, the Queen of Swords, for wisdom, clarity, and truthful speech.

Here's another example: I recently heard a friend of mine talking on a podcast. She stated that she would possibly carry the Emperor to a job interview as that's the energy she would embrace: fire element, strong, courageous, structured. I lack fire in my astrological makeup. Like my friend who would call in the Emperor for support for a job interview, I too require the leadership, courage, and confidence qualities that the Emperor brings. I always wear red to an interview, representing the fire element, which allows me to step into my own personal Emperor power. I often ask myself if wearing red, the color of fire and the color of the Emperor, is the reason I have gotten every job I have ever interviewed for that I truly wanted.

2

The Tarot Archetypes

The Queens' Council and the Major Arcana

In this chapter we will learn about the four queens and twenty-two major arcana archetypes within the tarot. Who are these archetypes, and what are their messages for you? What can you learn from them, and how can these archetypes work together to help you create your world and shift your energies for support during this year? These archetypal energies will bring you the power, strength, and guidance to move forward and become who you truly wish to be.

||||||||||||

Please note: This chapter contains many uses for essential oils. For a complete list of essential oils and precautions, see the appendix. Check precautions for each oil prior to making and using any blends due to possible skin irritations, and always dilute essential oils with a carrier oil before any contact with skin.

The Queens' Council

I love the queens of the tarot, who inspire rather than command and embody the elemental energy of the suit they are part of. Each queen represents a different elemental energy, and she can offer that energy for your personal support. When working with a queen, I like to encompass her energies by wearing her colors, speaking in her speech, wearing stones that support her energy, and creating a magical potion of her likeness to wear. This potion can be made up of oils, herbs, stones, and flower essences working harmoniously with one another to call in her energy, or you can choose one essential oil that encompasses her energy. I have personally found the queens to be a most successful companion and support for movement forward on my path. Create an altar for your queen, embrace her elemental energies, and let her support you.

Spending personal time with your chosen queen through imaginative journey—the state of allowing your mind and imagination to travel outside of yourself with a predetermined intention—is a powerful way to learn about her energies and receive a personal message. Sit with an image of your queen and a chosen essential oil. Choose any essential oil that you like. Breathe in the scent of the oil and allow yourself to truly connect with the scent. Breathe in the oil for a second time. Now ask your queen to speak with you. Ask her to show you all you need to know right now in this moment in time. Make sure you have your pen and paper ready to write down what you see, smell, feel, and hear. Really listen to what she has to tell you. In this chapter, I share each of my personal journeys with the four queens. Since these journeys are my personal journeys with the queens, please use these as a story, realizing that if you were to do your own personal imaginative journey, yours would be different. Doing your own imaginative journey would be a personal experience with the queen that only you could be a part of.

Let's take a look at each queen's story and energy for a better understanding of who she is. Each queen has an important message she wishes to tell. We start with the Queen of Pentacles.

The Queen of Pentacles

The Queen of Pentacles will support you when you are seeking to build a new foundation in your life. She will support the growth that manifests upon that foundation, and she will create the security and structure that is needed to support the abundance that stems from that foundation. The Queen of Pentacles will give you the nourishment and nurturing care to help you grow, reach out, and flourish. She will also teach you the importance of being the salt of the earth, to be reliable and always show up. Every task is important. Gratitude is important. The earth gives us our bounty so rejoice in the gifts of the mother and give back when you can.

Work with the Queen of Pentacles energy when you need to trust in who you are and what you have to say, for she will create a solidity in your body that pulls you back into your true nature. She will root you so that, like the mighty oak, you will grow to be strong for yourself and therefore you will become a grounding presence for those whom you know, love, and teach. You in turn will become their support. Allow the Queen of Pentacles to help you plant the seeds of business, finances, home, and family matters.

The Queen of Pentacles has helped me believe in myself many times when I have had self-doubt. I call upon her when I wish to be like the apple tree in the orchard, when I wish to bear fruit, for I know she will give me the ground in which to root, the nutrition that allows me to grow, and the support needed to bear fruit. She will give me all that I need to accomplish my goal.

Journey

I find myself in the living room of a home that feels as if it is nestled deep within the earth. It is dark inside this home, yet it is well-lit by lanterns. There is a sense of déjà vu happening. I am sure that this is not my first journey to this home. I feel at peace and very welcome here. The little home sits on a beautiful piece of land. The forest lies behind the house and in front there is an expansive golden meadow. I feel safe nestled in the softness of the dark green couch, surrounded by lots of hand-sewn yellow pillows. I smell cedar and oak. These are the beautiful woods within the home that create the walls and hardwood floors that now surround me.

As I let my eyes wander about the room, I notice the beautiful rugs on the floor that will be a comfort on a cold winter's night. In the middle of the room stands a grand and towering stone fireplace that is open on both sides, allowing for the warmth of the fire to reach every corner and every crevice in the room. There are stones of ruby, garnet, and onyx placed throughout the river rock in the fireplace as well as in the floor that surrounds it. To my right I can see the queen's throne. It is a high-back chair that is made from tree branches and twigs. Dark green and light yellow crystals hang from the branches of the chair and create an illusion of fireflies dancing about. A wise and elderly yellow tabby cat saunters slowly into the room with a grandness about her as if she is the creatrix of the sound that follows her. Grounding drums pound and cymbals chime as the sound carries itself deeper into the room. I begin to feel the vibration of sound move through the floor. As I open all my senses, I notice the scent of patchouli and know that she is near. I stand up to honor the Queen of Pentacles as she enters the room.

The queen stands before me. The energy shifts as she moves even closer. I feel her support and strength all around me, and I know that she has been with me for many lifetimes. The Queen of Pentacles has my back. She is kind and generous with her knowledge and support, and her grounding energy creates a solid foundation to stand upon. She is not a big woman, yet she is not a small woman either. She is sturdy and grounded in her body. Nutrition and health are important to her sense of well-being. Her bare feet touch the earth daily, and the tattooed vines that twist and wind around her arms are a symbol of the growth she can bring into one's life if allowed to do so. On her right arm, the vine continues down her forearm, twirling about until it stops at the nail bed of her first finger. She smiles at me and begins to speak.

> *I see the vine as a symbol of growth. The vine reminds me daily of how important it is to touch the earth and use my hands for the good of all. The earth is where we receive our nourishment and where we gain the knowledge of our ancestors. We are all made of earth. Earth is our home and our grounding. The element of earth can be found in the bones of our bodies, our support system. Take care of your bones, take care of your feet, and take care of all that supports your movement forward, whether that be of mind, body, or spirit. Nourish and respect your body, for it is the temple of your internal being, your soul. Remember to honor all four seasons by embracing the energies they have to offer. Give thanks for the changing of the seasons and give back to the earth. Winter is the time to honor the earth element as we step into our internal caves to rest and rejuvenate. This is the time to listen to the internal voice within and plan for the planting of seeds in the spring. The season of spring is when we will rise up with new vitality and a skip in our step. Be grateful for the ability to create with the gifts that grow and flourish beneath your feet. You are blessed as a living being upon the earth. Know this.*

The queen picks up a broom and begins to sweep.

> *Enjoy your daily tasks. Really throw yourself into what you are doing. All that you do is worth doing, from climbing a mountain to feeling the movement in the sweeping of a broom. Know your limitations and set boundaries, but when growth is needed, don't be afraid to step outside the box. It is important to know that you are worthy. Always remember to embrace your strengths and work through your challenges with a grounded intention. Always use your gifts wisely.*

The queen begins to speak again, but this time louder and with more authority, for her words relay an important message to me. This message resonates within my being, and again the words carry in them a slight familiarity. It is in that moment that I can confirm that she has been with me always and I have heard her voice before somewhere, possibly in a dream or another lifetime. She stands before me and looks deep within my eyes, with a sweet gaze of compassion.

> *I am here to remind you that you are rooted, like the tree, deeply within the earth. You are a part of this earth and like the tree, you must remember that the stars shine brightly for you every night. Allow yourself to expand and breathe. Allow yourself to grow. There will come a time when your youth is behind you. When you come to this time, I encourage you to honor yourself. Relax into your life and enjoy what you have sown into the world. Don't fight the aging process but don't allow yourself to decay before your time. You have gained the wisdom of your years; be proud of your knowledge. Remember your inner strength, and always remember to do your best and dig deep.*

She turns and walks through the door and out of the house. I now hold a new awareness. I am aware that I have the ability to call upon the Queen of Pentacles whenever the need or desire arises. I watch as she disappears down a long winding path until her physical body is gone from my view. Although I can no longer see her, I can still smell the scent of patchouli and I still hear her voice clearly as she speaks.

> *Remember me, for I am the Queen of Pentacles. Remember me when you feel lost or weak, for I am your grounding and I will help you gain knowledge and strength. I will help you move forward. Remember to be willing to ask for what you need in life. Ask and you will receive. I will gift you abundance, growth, and solidity. I remind you of who you are. You are a child of the earth who is worthy and needed in this world. I remind you, for I am the Queen of Pentacles.*

Creating an Altar

Use earth elemental energies for the Queen of Pentacles altar. This could include a bowl of salt, dirt, or earthy stones such as tiger's-eye, onyx, black or brown tourmaline, black kyanite, or Apache tears. Find stones that resonate with you.

Plant a seed and allow it to grow in a pot upon your altar table. Place a Queen of Pentacles card that speaks to you upon your altar. Use a green, brown, or black altar cloth. Set your blend or essential oil bottle upon the altar for three days prior to use to call in the queen's blessing upon the blend. Then begin to wear the scent and recite the mantra listed below. Do this for at least three times a day.

Light an earthy incense and ask your queen to walk with you through your day. Wear the colors of earth—black, brown, and green—and allow your jewelry to support the earth element through the stones used.

Mantra

I am strong. I am grounded. I am centered. I radiate abundance and growth. I hold deep within me the knowledge and wisdom of my ancestors. I am patient and I persevere. I am the Queen of Pentacles.

Essential Oils

Working with essential oils that ground and support growth such as vetiver, patchouli, cypress, clary sage, Spanish sage, Virginia cedarwood, and oakwood absolute will help call in the grounding support for your journey.

For more earth element essential oils, see the appendix.

Queen of Pentacles Magical Blend (Water Based)

This makes a spray you can use on your body or in the home.

INGREDIENTS

4-ounce glass spray bottle
Distilled water
Jojoba oil
Essential oils listed below

DIRECTIONS

- Add 1 teaspoon jojoba oil to the bottle.
- Add the following essential oils:
    18 drops Virginia cedarwood (*Juniperus virginiana*)
    16 drops vetiver (*Chrysopogon zizanioides*)
    15 drops cypress (*Cupressus sempervirens*)
    14 drops patchouli (*Pogostemon cablin*)
    11 drops juniper (*Juniperus communis*)
    11 drops clary sage (*Salvia sclerea*)
    7 drops sweet orange (*Citrus sinensis*)

- Fill bottle with distilled water.
- Blend by swirling the bottle's contents.
- Use up contents within two months.

Queen of Pentacles Magical Blend (Oil Based)

To create an oil blend, place the essential oils listed above in the bottle and then fill it with a carrier oil of your choice. For earth and water element oils, I often use almond oil as my base and then add a bit of jojoba to keep the oil from going rancid quickly. You now have a 4-ounce bottle of the oil blend that you can use to store and fill smaller roller bottles as you desire.

IIIIIIIIIIII

Note that almond oil should not be used by those with nut allergies. Work with camellia seed oil, fractionated coconut oil, or olive oil instead.

Simple Rituals with the Queen of Pentacles

- hiking
- gardening
- yoga
- dance
- earthing (bare feet upon the ground)
- gathering herbs and flowers
- cooking
- wearing black, brown, or green
- wearing earthy stones
- taking a salt bath

Planting a Seed

One of my favorite rituals for the earth element is to literally plant a seed and nourish it. Water and feed this seed, and as you nourish this seed, nourish yourself. Pamper yourself with healthy food, water, and movement. Dance for the seed and dance for yourself once per day as long as you are working with this queen. If for some reason the seed does not grow, plant a new seed.

Taking a Salt Bath

Salt baths help clear the aura, and adding essential oils can help you nurture yourself as well as have a newfound joy for self-care. The bath will lift your spirits as well as help ground and center you. Vinegar helps the body release toxins.

INGREDIENTS

    1 cup salt (Epsom, Dead Sea, or a combination)

    1 tablespoon jojoba oil

    3 drops Virginia cedarwood *(Juniperus virginiana)*

    2 drops patchouli *(Pogostermon cablin)*

    2 drops cypress *(Cupressus sempervirens)*

    ½ cup raw, unprocessed apple cider vinegar

    1 black onyx stone, raw and unpolished

DIRECTIONS

- Start running your bath water and get your desired temperature.
- Add the essential oils to your jojoba oil and pour into the bath.
- Mix salts in bath until they dissolve.
- Add the vinegar to your bath.
- Place onyx in the water.
- Soak for at least 10 minutes.
- Allow yourself to merge with the energies of the oils and stone.

- Repeat to yourself three times: "I am strong, I am grounded, I am healthy, I am whole and supported by the Mother."
- Feel your legs and spine being rooted into the earth. Breathe, relax, and enjoy.

Cooking

Since earth relates to winter, cook with roots and underground foods like turnips, potatoes, yams, and ginger. While ginger is a root and can relate to the earth element, it carries the energy of fire due to the heat it produces. This heat warms the body and helps heal and support your stomach and throat. Working with the earth element, you can also incorporate fire element foods. Fire will call in warmth and comfort during the winter season. Fire warms the body and soul. I think of chili with cayenne, baking with cinnamon and cardamom, hot drinks such as hot chocolate and earthy teas, homemade potato soup and anything comforting and warming.

EARTHY TEAS

- pu-erh
- rooibos
- honeybush

Choosing an earthy tea and adding your own spices to adjust the flavor is powerful magic. Possibly choose some vanilla or cocoa, which are both earth element; these spices will help ground you. Or maybe add some cinnamon, cardamom, ginger, or nutmeg, which call in the fire element and warm your bones. Not only does this help you ground, you are adding in a second element (fire) for support.

Grounding Meditation

Sit with both feet firm on the floor or earth. Sit with your spine straight and tall. Place your hands on your knees, palms facing upward to receive. Imagine roots growing from the bottom of your feet and reaching deep within the earth, all the way down, as far as the lava within the center of the earth.

Now imagine those roots reaching up into your body, all the way up, till they reach your heart. Feel green vines growing from your body and reaching out for all that life has to offer.

Now place a drop of your essential oil or blend upon your feet, your heart, and the palm of your hands to indicate you are open to receiving the bounties of the earth. If you are working with a straight essential oil rather than a blend and you have not diluted the oil, then just inhale the oil rather than placing it upon your body. You will receive the same effect.

Recite the Queen of Pentacles mantra and move on throughout your day knowing that you are grounded, safe, and protected by our Mother Earth and her tarot representative, the Queen of Pentacles.

The Queen of Cups

The Queen of Cups calls in a gentle flow of healing within your life. She supports your spiritual development, heart energy, love, and compassion, as well as difficult emotions, healing, friendship, community, intuition, and the mysteries of the unknown. This queen is psychic and full of secrets and magical flow. Call upon this queen when you feel blocked by emotions or require support to move through emotions. Call upon her when you want to bring love into your life or find a like-minded community. Call upon her when you wish to see in the dark, trusting your intuition and psychic abilities as you move forward on your path. Call upon this queen when an idea or creative project wishes to be born. Think of pregnant waters and the birth of your creative spirit.

When I am not being compassionate with myself or others, I work with the Queen of Cups. She gives me the confidence to keep moving when I am beating myself up or when I need to trust my intuition and seek my own counsel for answers. I call upon her for the magic of the nighttime and the mysteries within.

Journey

It is a dark and rainy night, and I am hunkered down in my little attic room. I love this little room, especially on a night like this one, because of the metal roof on the house: I can hear the sound of the rain tap, tap, tapping above my head, and this has a very calming effect upon me. I have lightened up the space with lots of candles and a couple of lanterns, and it looks quaint. There is a small table in the middle of the room with large comfy pillows all around it. I have decided to spend my evening sitting on the pillows, listening to the rain, and drinking some hot tea—a white peony tea with rose and lavender. This will definitely calm my nerves and relax me for the evening.

I sit down and take a sip of tea, then place pillows all around me for support as I lean my head back against the wall just to relax and listen to the rain. I am all alone, except for the sound of the rain and the flickers of the candles. I have felt emotional all day with memories of friends, family, and pets that have long since been removed from my life, some through death and some just because of life circumstances. I am realizing that time seems to get away from me and now I was wondering where they had gone—friends, family, pets, and time. There was a shift happening in me. I could feel it. After sixty years upon this earth, I was changing yet again. What was this shift that was happening, and where was it taking me? The energy in my life was unclear, mysterious, and yet exciting. I was about to step into the unknown, and this evening felt like an initiation for transformation.

I closed my eyes for a while and just listened. I began to cry, not having a specific reason for the tears yet feeling they were necessary for this shift to occur in me. I allowed myself to cry, and I allowed the tears to cleanse and purify my heart. I was about to doze off into a deep sleep when all of a sudden the rain started coming down heavily on the roof. The raindrops sounded larger and more powerful. When the sound of the drops upon the roof took on the rhythmic sound of drums, there was almost a hypnotizing effect on my body. I imagined myself moving to the drums and allowing the rain to magically fall upon my face and body. The more I moved, the more entranced I became and the more beautiful I felt. After a while I began to realize that I was not dancing alone. I had a partner. I opened my eyes to see a beautiful woman gently dancing to the rhythm of the rain and smiling at me. I also noticed that she wore a crown upon her head. I decided to stop dancing and bow before this beautiful queen. She lifted my head and said, "I am so proud of you. You are finally coming into your power. Do you feel the shift?"

She took my hand as we both sat down upon the pillows. She poured herself a cup of tea and took a sip. "I hope you don't mind," she said, "I could not resist the scent of the tea; I had to have a taste." She looked at me and began to speak.

> *You are releasing many emotions right now, and this is healing. You are letting go of guilt, anger, jealousy, pain, and resentment. You are healing. You have forgiven yourself and you are forgiving others. This will help you to step into who you truly are, and I am so happy for you. Let the tears flow. Never, ever dam them up. Unreleased emotions can create a blockage in your energy flow, and in time this blockage will burst. It is best to let the tears heal you; it is best to let it all flow through you and out of you. This is what is happening for you. Open your heart like the top of the cup and be open to receive. Now you have room for the gifts that are available to you.*

I take a moment to allow myself to gaze upon her beauty. She is a small woman with long black hair that comes to her waist. She has silver running through her hair, and her hair is braided on top and pulled back to create a small bun in the back of her head. She wears silver rings, silver earrings, and she has a rose quartz necklace that resembles a chain of small roses stretching around her neck.

I wear these little roses to express compassion for the world and for those who have been gifted the ability to walk upon the earth and be present at this time. The rose quartz is a symbol for love and compassion. I always carry love and compassion with me, as should you. You never know when you will need them. Share your emotions with others and be truthful with your feelings. Remember that tears are healing and cleansing. Acknowledge and release, for this is the key to well-being.

The rain starts to mellow out and we only hear a light constant tap, tap, tap on the roof. The storm has passed. She looks directly at me and says:

The memories that were with you today were memories of love. When we take the time to remember those who were a part of our lives, we bring forth love. It is courageous to remember, it is beautiful to remember, and through remembering we see the power and courage of those who have touched our souls and taught us our lessons. You are opening your heart to the beauty of the human relationship. At times we have seen this beauty in the world through those who have been willing to step out and share what is in their hearts. At times we have watched those who are not afraid, those who have the courage to lead with compassion and love rather than hate and anger. We all have that courage. Do not let fear be your guide. Follow the voice within and allow your intuition to lead the way. You, my friend, can see in the dark if you just trust, and with trust in your heart you will always find your way through the forest. Welcome your true voice into your reality.

Tonight we have the gift of water. We hear the water on the rooftop, and you have felt the cleansing water of your tears. Always remember that water is the first ingredient added into the cauldron. We are born out of water, and water is where we birth our creations. Stir and conjure your dreams into reality. When you use your emotions and tears to create your magic, you have a power that will be a force to reckon with. You are putting all of yourself into your spell, your wish, your intention. Send love, healing, and compassion out to the world through the power of water. Just let it flow.

As the energy again shifts in the room, I realize how late it has gotten and I feel that my time with this magical queen is almost over. I finish my tea and look at the Queen of Cups with joy in my eyes for the time I have had with her. This too will be a memory—a memory that I will always carry with me. As I stand, the Queen of Cups places a beautiful rose quartz ring upon my finger and speaks a powerful message to me.

Wear this ring as a reminder of the power of love and the power of water. Know that water gives the gift of life. Nothing lives without the element of water. Your body is mainly water. Water cleanses and purifies. Embrace and drink in the beauty of your life. Share your dreams, trust your intuition, and step out and away from fear. Always be willing to give, and always be open to receive.

She turns to walk away. Although no words are spoken, I can hear her closing message in my mind.

Call upon me when you feel lost and alone. Call upon me when you feel love, when you encounter fear, when you find confusion, anger, or pain stepping into your life. Call upon me when you need compassion or need to be compassionate. Call upon me when you don't feel like you belong, when you feel left out and left behind. Call upon me when you are too deeply seated within the dark cave of self. Call upon me when you feel held too close, when you can't break free, and I will teach you to flow.

Now there is nothing but silence. The rain has stopped, the candles still dance, and I can no longer see the queen, yet I know she is still near and always will be. All I have to do is to ask for her presence and be open to receive.

Creating an Altar

The Queen of Cups relates to the element of water, so I like to place a small bowl of rose water upon my altar. The bowl, like the cup, is open to receive, and the rose water is a sacred scent to this queen. Place some heart-shaped stones upon your altar, or stones such as aquamarine, blue lace agate, amazonite, blue aragonite, chrysocolla, emerald, blue opal, pink opal, rose quartz, or rhodochrosite to embrace her energy.

The Queen of Cups also appreciates flowers placed nearby. Use a blue, green, or pink cloth to dress the table. Place a favorite Queen of Cups card in the center to create a powerful devotion to this queen.

Place your oil blend or a single essential oil upon the altar for three days prior to use. Then begin to wear or breathe in the scent and recite the mantra listed below. Do this at least three times a day. Wear watery colors like blue, blue-green, or silver.

Mantra

I am grateful for the flow of love and harmony in my life.
My cup runneth over with the gifts of compassion, joy, and
grace. My intuition always guides me, and my heart is
open to receive. I am the Queen of Cups.

Essential Oils

Work with a heart-based sweet essential oil such as jasmine, rose,
vanilla, rose geranium, ylang-ylang, myrtle, lemon, or clary sage to
support the energies of the Queen of Cups.

For more water element essential oils, see the appendix.

Queen of Cups Magical Blend (Water Based)

This makes a spray you can use on your body or in the home.

INGREDIENTS

4-ounce glass spray bottle
Distilled water
Jojoba oil
Essential oils listed below

DIRECTIONS

- Add 1 teaspoon jojoba oil to the bottle.
- Add the following essential oils:
    13 drops ylang-ylang *(Cananga odoranta)*
    10 drops vanilla *(Vanilla planifolia)*
    10 drops rose geranium *(Pelargonium graveolens)*
    9 drops myrtle *(Myrtus communis)*
    3 drops thyme *(Thymus vulgaris)*
    5 drops lemon *(Citrus limon)*
    3 drops rose *(Rosa damascena)*

- Fill bottle with distilled water.
- Blend by swirling the bottle's contents.
- Use up contents within two months.

Queen of Cups Magical Blend (Oil Based)

To create an oil blend, place the oils listed above into a 4-ounce bottle and fill it with a carrier oil of your choice. For earth and water oils, I use almond oil as my base and then add a bit of jojoba to keep the blend from going rancid. You now have 4 ounces of the blend, which you can store and fill smaller roller bottles as you desire. Cap and store in a dark space.

> Note that almond oil should not be used by those with nut allergies. Work with camellia seed oil, fractionated coconut oil, or olive oil instead.

Simple Rituals with the Queen of Cups

- drinking water
- bathing or showering
- being near water
- swimming

Tea Drinking Ritual

Grab your favorite magical cup. Make a tea of your choice. Sit in silence and hold the cup within your hands. Feel the warmth and loving support from the cup. Take a moment to be thankful for all you have been given. Feel blessed and open to receive. Think of this cup as a vessel of love and compassion. Speak into the cup. Give it your prayers, wishes, and desires. Allow the energies to merge with the tea. Then drink, allowing all to seep into your being. You have stated your wishes to the universe and embodied the energies within yourself.

Watery Teas

Green teas relate to the element of water. Jasmine green tea is the perfect drink for the Queen of Cups. You can choose the green tea of your choice and add in some floral notes by adding chamomile, rose, lavender, and jasmine flowers to the blend, or you can purchase a premade blend with green tea and floral notes.

A Water Bottle Ritual

Think about what you wish and desire to bring into your life. For example, if you have a chronic health issue, you can ask the Queen of Cups to help dissolve the blocked energy within your body that could be causing pain and discomfort. Get specific and dream big. Pull out your favorite water bottle. You can decorate the water bottle or just get a piece of masking tape and write the wish across it. Affix the tape or the images to the water bottle. When you drink from it, you are receiving the message on the bottle. Every time you take a drink, you will remember what you are calling into your life—literally drink and embody your desired energy. I once drank in internal beauty for a whole month. I felt more positive and kind to myself, and I also improved my internal belief in who I am as a being upon the earth. Try drinking in love, compassion, self-care, or anything you desire.

Taking a Salt Bath

Salt baths help to clear the aura and call in new energies. I like to work with Roman chamomile, myrtle, rose, or a combination of the three for the Queen of Cups. You can even add a tea, like chamomile, into your bath water. This aids with relaxation and soothes and comforts your body. Brew a pot of double-strong tea and allow it to cool, then pour into bath water. Purchase a bath bag for actual herbs like chamomile flowers or rose petals. This keeps the herbs and flowers contained so they don't muck up your bath.

Separate from your bath bag, to 1 cup of salts add 1 tablespoon jojoba oil that has had 5 drops of Roman chamomile essential oil and 1 drop of rose essential oil added to it. (The salts act as a carrier and help disperse the oils into the water so they don't just stick to the side of the tub.) Add oil and salt mixture to your running bath water.

Keep in mind when taking a bath or shower that you are not just taking a shower; you are cleansing and purifying your body and spirit. Ask your guides and angels to help with the wash so you bring in new joy and health. Add stones like aquamarine, blue lace agate, blue calcite, rose quartz, or other heart energy or water element stones. Relax and enjoy your magical bath. Imagine yourself as the cup: open to receive.

If you want to take a shower, take the desired oils and add them into 1 tablespoon jojoba oil, then add them to a salt or sugar base. Add extra carrier oil to make the salt scrub wet. This creates a salt scrub you can rub on your body during the shower.

ΙΙΙΙΙΙΙΙΙΙΙΙ

For the salt scrub, do not use Epsom salts; use fine Dead Sea salt. Do not use a salt scrub after shaving or anywhere you have a wound.

The Queen of Wands

The Queen of Wands is fire. She supports our passions, our desires, the spark within, magic, creativity, leadership, transformation, and change. I often call in this queen as I only have the element of fire in one house of my astrological chart. The Queen of Wands brings you courage, desire, and charisma. She supports your movement outward. She helps you shed the old to make way for the new. This queen is a leader, and she helps you light the spark in yourself and others. Like moths to the flame, she stimulates others to be attracted to your internal flame. Light candles for this queen and bask in her power.

I also like to work with the Queen of Wands when I create spells and magic, for she is well versed in this area. Think of fire as the ability to expand your energies outward. The Queen of Wands will help to support these outward-moving energies as well as transformation and change.

Journey

When I wake up in the mornings, usually the first thought on my mind is tea. This was especially true on this particular morning. I hadn't slept well and I needed the comfort and warmth of my morning tea to stir up some energy. I had a lot on my mind, and anxiety had managed to creep into my night and keep me from sleeping. I was really tired, yet I had so much to do. I made my way downstairs and put the tea kettle on. I had recently created a new blend of tea that I called "a cup of fire." It is a lovely blend of black tea, cardamom, cinnamon, nutmeg, ground ginger, turmeric, and black pepper. I would brew this up and then add a bit of coconut almond milk to lighten the tea blend and make it creamy. It is quite a delicious blend, with so many healing properties both physical and magical. My day does not begin without the warmth of a teacup in my hands.

I sat with my tea and thought about the work I needed to get done. I was getting ready for my biggest event ever. I was speaking and vending at an upcoming tarot conference, and it was now only two months away. There is so much to do for an event like this, especially when you are both speaking and vending. With this event, I was allowing myself to truly be seen for the first time. I had spoken at events before, but this one was different. I was sharing my personal creation with the world this time, not just teaching about what someone else had created. This was mine; this was me. I had my mind set on total perfection and was hard driven to do the best I possibly could in preparation. Inside I felt so much excitement yet so much fear. What if I was not good enough? What if I forgot my place and lost my way in my presentation? What if everyone else thought my creation was nonsense, illogical, and totally unbelievable? Yet I believed in my work and I believed in myself, so what was the problem? Since I had chosen to call in all of these fire spices this morning, I knew that I needed to sit quiet for a while and call in support from the Queen of Wands. Who better to lift my spirits and ignite the passion within me?

I closed my eyes and asked for her permission to speak with her. I had been gifted the blessing of her presence before. This would not be the first time I have asked for her help. I sat and waited and allowed my imagination to take over. This would help me form my questions for the queen. As expected, my mind began to let go, and I knew what questions to ask of her. How can I create a powerful, enchanting and accessible presentation that reaches and touches my audience? How can I truly allow myself to be seen? How do I step out of the energy of fear? I felt these questions were a good foundation to start from.

I took a deep breath and reached for my essential oil blend of cinnamon, orange, black pepper, cedarwood, vetiver, cardamom, and rose oils. I sprayed the blend in the air three times and took a deep breath, focusing on my questions for the queen. Again, I let my imagination take over and with pen in hand I wrote down whatever I heard within my mind, whatever I smelled, and whatever feelings I felt in my body. All of my senses were open, and I was ready to receive her message.

I felt her enter the room and place her hand upon my shoulder. I could feel her support radiate throughout my body and then ground beneath my feet. I felt loved. She came and sat before me and began to speak. The first words out her mouth were these:

I am proud of you. You have chosen to step forward and allow yourself to be seen. Now that you have chosen this path, you cannot run and you cannot hide. This is no longer an option for you. It is not the time to shrink with fear; it is the time to shine like the sun. You have been gifted with a lesson for the world. It is important to share this lesson, this message, and now is the time to do so. You would not have received the message yourself if you were not the one to relay it to others. You were chosen for this. You created it, and now only you can express the full message to the world. You must stand up with integrity and be grateful for what you have been given.

I now understood that she would not let me back down. She wanted me to stand my ground and be powerful. Wow, I never think of myself as powerful. I may be compassionate and I always try to be kind, but I would not use the word powerful. I knew she had read my mind when she began to speak again.

Yes, you are compassionate and kind. That much is true, but there is another truth, and that is that you are powerful. I will help you learn to embrace this quality. I offer you now not only the word powerful, I offer you leadership, passion, the spark, and charisma. You need not be afraid when you embody my personal qualities. I will make you courageous and strong. I know you believe in yourself and I believe in you, so let us create the you that others can believe in. This can be achieved with confidence, courage, and charisma. Let your passion come through when you speak. Let your audience see the spark within you, and you will in turn ignite the spark within them. Don't forget to wear some red, even if it is only on your lips. Don't forget to stand tall and accept this gift you have been given with joy in your heart. The Sun shines upon you now. Accept the gift and share it with others. Who do you wish to see in the mirror? Create her. I am with you, so embody me, and as you embody me, I embody you. In

*time these fire qualities of mine will become natural to you
and you will be powerful; know this to be true.*

She looked at me again and said,

*I believe I have answered all your questions. Now go and
make an altar in my honor. Not only will you honor me
in this way, but the altar will be a daily reminder of our
conversation. You will begin to embrace this new you. You
will become empowered by just knowing that I am with
you. Again, remember that I am proud of you. Be proud of
yourself, yet keep your qualities of compassion and kind-
ness. The world needs a bit of love right now so share your
compassion. It will be well accepted.*

In a puff of smoke, she was gone. I have not forgotten her message
and I continue to wear red lipstick, drink my cup of fire tea, and
wear my essential oil blend daily. I am on my way, and fear is not
welcome on this journey.

Creating an Altar

The Queen of Wands embodies the fire element, so start off by placing a red, yellow, or orange cloth upon your altar. Place as many candles as you can safely on the altar. Add stones like red carnelian, fire
agate, amber, citrine, fire opal, sunstone, flint—any red and orange
stones. Keep bowls of spice like cinnamon, ginger, black pepper, and
cayenne upon your altar.

I keep a small cauldron on my Queen of Wands altar. I light candles and burn herbs in it for her pleasure. Place your favorite Queen
of Wands card upon the altar to show her beauty. Set your fire oil
blend or designated essential oil bottle upon the altar for three days
prior to use to call in the queen's blessing upon the blend or oil. Then
begin to wear or breathe in the scent and recite the mantra listed
below. Do this for at least three times a day. Light a spicy incense

and ask your queen to walk with you through your day. Wear the colors of fire—red, yellow, and orange—and allow your jewelry to support the fire element through the stones used.

Mantra

I am passion, desire, and the creative spark within. I am courage, fearless in the face of change. I am the creator of my life. I am magic. I am the Queen of Wands.

Essential Oils

Working with fire element oils can assist with your connection to the Queen of Wands. Oils such as cinnamon, frankincense, black pepper, ginger, orange, lime, tangerine, basil, fennel, anise, and angelica seed oil give off the same energy as the queen.

For more fire element essential oils, see the appendix.

Queen of Wands Magical Blend (Water Based)

This makes a spray you can use on your body or in the home.

Ingredients

4-ounce glass spray bottle

Distilled water

Jojoba oil

Essential oils listed below

Directions

- Add 1 teaspoon jojoba oil to the bottle.
- Add the following essential oils:
    16 drops Virginia cedarwood *(Juniperus virginiana)*
    7 drops ginger *(Zingiber officinale)*
    18 drops coriander *(Coriandrum sativam)*
    9 drops black pepper *(Piper nigrum)*

10 drops petitgrain *(Citrus aurantium)*

8 drops cardamom *(Elettaria cardamomum)*

21 drops lime *(Citrus aurantifolia)*

21 drops sweet orange oil *(Citrus sinensis)*

10 drops rose *(Rosa damascena)*

- Fill bottle with distilled water.
- Blend by swirling the bottle's contents.
- Use up contents within two months.

Queen of Wands Magical Blend (Oil Based)

To create an oil blend, place the essential oils in a 4-ounce bottle that can be capped and fill it with a carrier oil of your choice. For fire elemental oils, I use sunflower oil as my base and then add a bit of jojoba to keep the oil from going rancid. You now have a 4-ounce bottle of the oil that you can use to store and fill smaller roller bottles as you desire. Keep stored in a dark area.

Simple Rituals with the Queen of Wands

- lighting candles
- bonfire
- eating spicy food
- sex
- passionate dance

The Cauldron Within Ritual

This cauldron sits in your diaphragm area. It represents your will to become. I imagine this cauldron in my belly, boiling with steam that moves upward toward the heavens. The steam carries my desires and my creative spark. In this cauldron we have water within and fire below. I place my desires—all that calls me—and the image of who I wish to be inside the water. Anything I am longing for goes into the pot.

Anything I no longer need in my life I put in the flames beneath the cauldron to be composted. This is like a prayer being requested while all that must go is released at the same time. When you meditate, breathe through the fire under the cauldron. You are the creatrix of the fire. Allow yourself to become that fire. Create the outward-moving energy.

Allow the fire to burn and the cauldron to boil until you feel the ritual is complete. Repeat daily for nine days.

Candle Magic

Performing candle magic is a wonderful way to work with fire and manifest your desires while banishing unwanted energies. The power of transformation is our friend. Select the color of the candle that resonates with you and represents your desire. I use green for money, silver for spirituality, black to banish, pink for love, red for passion, orange for joy, and white for connecting with my guides and angels. Use a small candle for fast magic and a larger candle for slow-moving magic. You will need to completely burn the candle down, so larger candles may require a daily burn. You can write a message or a name on the candle and dress the candle with an elemental oil blend or a fire-based essential oil.

Use a fire oil for passion, desires, or change. Use a water oil for love, community, or spirituality. Use an air oil for communication such as writing, speaking, or singing, as well as for truth and clarity. Use an earth oil for grounding, abundance, health, fertility, and money.

I often write a mantra to go with my spell. Sometimes I use nursery rhymes and change the words. "Connie, Connie, go away; no, you can't come back to play" is an example of a banishing mantra. Say it, write it, or sing it many times a day. This is powerful magic that can aid you on your path. You can find more information on writing your own mantra in chapter 8.

Drinking Tea

Black teas relate to the fire element. Add in spicy herbs like ginger, cinnamon, star anise, nutmeg, and cardamom. Add a dash of honey and a milk of your choice.

The Queen of Swords

The Queen of Swords embodies the element of air. She brings the gifts of clarity, truth, communication, swiftness, and getting things done correctly, with focus and attention to detail. This queen also carries the energy of inspiration and new ideas. Call upon this queen when you need to speak your truth and be clear about your thoughts. Call upon her when you need to communicate via writing, singing, speaking, or just want to have an honest conversation. Call upon her when you need to find clarity or make a clear decision. The Queen of Swords cuts through the muck and makes things clear. She does not mess around with her words. Sometimes her words can cut you like a knife. Honesty, integrity, and truth are key to the Queen of Swords.

The Queen of Swords is the least emotional queen in the tarot. When emotions are out of control, this queen helps bring clarity to what is going on. She allows you to release the feelings that get in the way of logical thinking. The Queen of Swords asks you to breathe clarity into your life.

Journey

What do you still hold on to that no longer serves your truth? What is holding you back due to these falsehoods that you still carry with you? What is the one thing that you remember that has scarred you? These are the questions that came into my mind as I stepped into the meadow of my imagination. The meadow is my place to connect. Whenever I want to connect with my ancestors, angels, and guides, I step into the meadow. I step into the meadow every time I do a tarot reading for someone or even if I just want some peace and quiet. I know I can find it in the meadow. I went to the meadow this morning just for that, some peace and quiet, yet these questions were placed in my mind as I entered the field. Where did they come from? They must be important. I could tell that one of my guides was asking me these questions and they were being asked for a reason.

I found my way to the center of the meadow and took a seat on the pillows that lay there waiting for me. I have what you might call a meadow oasis setup. Pillows and a table situated under a large canopy and fresh running water in the little stream that runs nearby. The meadow is surrounded by woods, and there is a meeting stone for conversations. The meeting stone is a large rock where my guides, angels, and ancestors will wait for me to arrive for our conversation. We talk about life, and they share their wisdom with me when needed. On this day I sat in the little oasis, calling in peace and waiting to see who would pop in to discuss these questions that have been laid upon the talk table. Often my first glimpse of the guest for the day will come in the form of an animal. For Herne the Hunter, one of my guides, I will first see a stag in the field. In the case of my grandmother Edna, it is a brown rabbit or hare. This is not a little bunny; it is a rabbit. Today I spot an eagle flying high in the sky, and a hawk lands near my feet and gazes up at me. Today I am meeting with the Queen of Swords. The hawk is her animal companion and she is the eagle in the sky, flying circles around me. She lands upon the meeting stone as the eagle and then shapeshifts into the Queen of Swords. She is beautiful and grand. She is dressed in royal blue, and her long hair seems to blow in the breeze that is not there. She sits upon the stone, places her sword upon her lap, and beckons me toward her.

I sit beneath the stone and look up to her with focused intention. I am grateful for the opportunity to receive this lesson from her. I sit in silence as she speaks.

> *It is now time to let go of old, repetitive thoughts and patterns that cause self-doubt. These thoughts and patterns hide your truth. They keep you bound by not allowing you to reach your full potential. You must break free from the bondage of the mind. Now tell me, what is the one memory that has scarred you? This is often the beginning of all the self-destruction that follows you throughout your life. Often this is too painful for some to talk about, but sometimes it is something someone said that has stuck with you. Words are power. I believe that the latter is your situation. Is this true? So tell me, how did this all start for you?*

I tell her the story of my third-grade year in elementary school. I had changed schools for one year in the second grade and then returned to my previous school in the third grade. In my memory we are at the teacher's conference and my teacher was speaking to my parents. Life had been difficult in the previous year, as my dad was in the army and had been sent to Vietnam. He had been gone for a long time, it seemed, and when he returned I was so happy to have him home. Maybe the year he was gone had taken a toll on me. I listened as my teacher spoke to my parents and I heard her say, "Your daughter is struggling with the lessons this year. I don't know if extra work would help her because I just do not believe she will ever be able to keep up with the other children. I do not believe she can grasp and learn these lessons in time. She will always be behind."

This statement broke my heart. I felt I was doing well under the circumstances. It was like a punch in the stomach. The takeaway for me was what I had heard in my mind—Your daughter is just not smart enough. She will never be as bright as the other children. Even though my teacher did not say those exact words, this is what registered in my mind. I continued my life with this belief, never allowing myself to be truly seen and never trying hard or playing all my cards because I believed I would only be let down.

The Queen of Swords stood and held her sword above her head.

We are now going to cut through this mucky untruth and make things clear for you. You will let go of this dishonoring belief about yourself.

All of a sudden, she swung her sword above my head. The sword's swing was so powerful that I could feel its movement through the air, almost as if the hawk had just flown by in place of the sword.

This will destroy those thought patterns, but you must be willing to do the work to keep those thoughts at bay. You must never accept those words as your truth ever again.

I bowed to her in acceptance of her statement.

Now that you no longer believe in this untruth, you are set free. All other examples of self-doubt should be tested for their validity. If something calls to you, then do it. You cannot say you can't if you have never tried, can you? You are stopping your own flow and denying your true gifts. Self-denial creates fear and anxiety, and you resist your own movement forward. Now, I am not saying that you can never be defeated because some things can and will defeat you. We cannot be and do everything in this lifetime. We must choose our path forward, and through this choice we must have the courage to follow through and not allow self-doubt to be involved. We are all powerful in our own unique ways. Always remember that life is the consistent movement of energy shifting and changing as it moves. You can literally reach out and change the energy. You can create new flow. This is magic. Feel that soft breeze upon your face? That is life. It is all around you.

She asked me to kneel, and I did so. She placed her sword upon my lap and said,

We all have swords, and we are all queens. What is a sword but a tool, a weapon? Now use this sword to bring clarity into your life. Think of this sword as logic. Clear away untruth, and don't let your emotions cloud you. At times we must look at things logically. We must use the sword to get to the truth of the matter. Know this.

In an instant, she was gone and I was alone sitting in the meadow. This was a powerful lesson today from the Queen of Swords—one I will always remember. As I started to walk back out of the meadow, I carried my new sword home with me.

Creating an Altar

Choose a blue, white, purple, or silver altar cloth to cover your table. You need incense for the Queen of Swords. Incense drifts our messages up to the heavens, so sending your clear request to the Queen of Swords via the smoke gets her attention. Place crystals such as amethyst, clear quartz, azurite, diamond, fluorite, turquoise, and kyanite on the altar. Symbols of birds, feathers and bone, are also appropriate. Find your favorite image of the Queen of Swords and place it in the center of the space to honor this queen. Set your blend or essential oil bottle upon the altar for three days prior to use to call in the queen's blessing upon the blend or oil. Then begin to wear or breathe in the scent and recite the mantra listed below. Do this for at least three times a day for thirty days. Light any scents that remind you of the wind, if able, and ask the queen to walk with you through your day. Wear the colors of air: white, silver, purple, and light blue. Accessorize with coordinating jewelry to support the air element.

Mantra

I am a cool breeze, and I see clearly. I speak my truth with confidence. I know who I am and where I am going. I get things done correctly and in a timely manner. I cut through the muck with my sword to bring clarity. I am the Queen of Swords.

Essential Oils

Work with air-based oils such as lavender, peppermint, spearmint, corn mint, eucalyptus, lemongrass, citronella, marjoram, oregano, and tarragon. They can help bring in the essence of the Queen of Swords.

For more air essential oils, see the appendix.

Queen of Swords Magical Blend (Water Based)

This makes a spray you can use on your body or in the home.

INGREDIENTS

4-ounce glass spray bottle
Jojoba oil
Distilled water
Essential oils listed below

DIRECTIONS

- Add 1 teaspoon jojoba oil to the bottle.
- Add the following essential oils:
    21 drops lavender *(Lavendula angustifolia)*
    15 drops tangerine *(Citrus reticulata)*

11 drops eucalyptus *(Eucalyptus globulus)*

10 drops peppermint *(Mentha x piperita)*

8 drops lemongrass *(Cymbopogon citratus)*

8 drops marjoram *(Origamum majorana)*

- Fill bottle with distilled water.
- Blend by swirling the bottle's contents.
- Use up contents within two months.

Queen of Swords Magical Blend (Oil Based)

Use a 4-ounce glass bottle with a capped top. To create an oil, place the essential oils listed above in the bottle and fill it with a carrier oil of your choice. For air element oils, I use sunflower oil as my base and I then add a bit of jojoba to keep the oil from going rancid. You now have a 4-ounce bottle of the oil that you can use to store and fill smaller roller bottles as you desire. Store bottles in a dark area.

Simple Rituals with the Queen of Swords

- breathing exercises
- meditation
- burning incense
- journaling
- singing
- writing

Walking Air Meditation

One of my favorite ways to work with the Queen of Swords is air walking. It isn't as hard as it sounds. Go outside and walk. As you move, allow your body to truly feel the air on your skin. Take three deep breaths and walk slowly; you want to give yourself time to really feel the air surrounding you. Imagine this air going through your body. As you walk, let all the gunk and blockages within your being be pushed out of your body by the air. Leave a trail of unwanted energies and stuff behind you. You are releasing all that needs to go in order to create a new clarity in your life.

Letter to the Queen

Write a letter to the Queen of Swords. Ask for help to lead you to your desired outcome. This can help generate ideas and bring clear thought to your process. Be honest; it will get her attention.

Is it clarity, truth, study, inspiration, or the strength to organize that you need help with? State your desired outcome and ask her for guidance. As issues come up on your journey, continue to write to the queen, asking for more assistance and inspiration. She will be there.

Burn Incense Daily

Light incense to the Queen of Swords and your guides, angels, and ancestors every morning when you get up. This creates a group effort to support your needs. Say a prayer and give thanks for the support you receive once the smoke begins to flow. Be grateful as well as truthful and honest about your needs. Start your day off by doing this and a five-minute meditation to hold the energy of gratitude. Ask for the help of your support group often, as they cannot assist without you asking.

The Major Arcana

Below you will find the descriptions along with the correspondences for the twenty-two major arcana cards as well as their corresponding plant energies. You may notice that not all of the correspondences between the major arcana card and its chosen plant ally line up the same. You will find in my plant descriptions that I have given the explanation as to why I chose each plant for each major arcana card, and the reasons vary. Sometimes the planetary influences line up and sometimes they do not. Sometimes the elements line up and sometimes they do not. I hope I have explained my reasoning well in order to give a clear understanding to my choice of plant ally.

In some of the descriptions of the card energies, I have given a personal example of my experiences with the card or an example of a family, friend, or client who has experienced the card's energy. You will not find these examples with every major arcana card because I personally have not experienced that year's energy in my life or I don't have an experience to share from a friend or client. I have only written about what has been experienced in reality by myself or as an example given to me by someone who has experienced that energy personally. We do not always move through all of these energies individually in our lifetime. It may be fun to calculate your personal years from the past and see how those major arcana cards played a part during that time in your life.

You will also find a scent description for each essential oil, along with its planetary or astrological influence, its elemental energy and its magical properties.

In the appendix you will find additional information on the essential oil, such as the Latin name, how the plant was processed, the plant part used, scent grouping, blending note, and precautions. Always check precautions prior to using any essential oil.

The Fool

NUMBER: 0 or 22 (often considered both or neither)
ELEMENT: Air
PLANETARY INFLUENCE: Uranus

A Message from the Fool

I step off, falling into the clouds—falling, falling, and falling until I stumble upon a soft bed of clover, where I sleep until the sun awakens me with my first breath.

Are you ready to jump or have you already taken the leap of faith? What new beginnings stir within you? What is it that wishes to be born? Go ahead: be free and allow yourself to fly, but keep your wits about you. Remember that you do seek the ground eventually, so set your roots deep within your soul so that your spirit may fly.

It is not in the past and it is not in the future; it is in the here and now. What is it that is calling you, and where are you going? Be clear and step wisely, for it is time to move forward. Life's taking you on a journey. Take a deep breath and leap!

Meanings

The Fool represents our soul, our spirit. The Fool is the archetype of our divine self as it makes the decision, the leap of faith, to step into human form. This is our desire to experience life. The Fool is with us each time we take a leap throughout our journey of humanness. Each time we make the decision to step into something new or unfamiliar—something that we feel innocent in, a new beginning—the Fool walks with us. Think of leaving home for college, the step into marriage, choosing our career, the purchase of a new home, entering into any type of new relationship or creative endeavor. The Fool enters our life each time we choose to be different or daring.

Although the outcome is unknown, we still leap because there is an internal knowing, an internal truth, that this is where we have chosen to go.

The Fool is the dreamer, the one who follows his dreams without hesitation. The Fool is the seed in that he represents unlimited possibilities and potential. I like to think of Peter Pan, one of my favorite characters in literature: he is not afraid, yet he is innocent and at the same time boastful and full of ego and will. Courage and wonderment abound from his frolicking energy as he moves forward on his journey.

If you have chosen the Fool or the Fool has chosen you, it is a time to trust in your internal knowing and step off the cliff. Each time we are the Fool, we are stepping into something new, something we know deep within our being is the next step we must take. There is a sense of innocence and freedom, and you are open to receive.

Anything is possible, and there is a belief in self. It is almost as if your spirit is at work, guiding you on your path, and before you take that step off the cliff, your spirit speaks and states, "You know this is the next step on your path; take it." You have all the tools required to help you find your way as well as all the knowledge of your ancestors and your past lives within you. The Fool is the guiding force within each one of us that encourages movement into the next passage of our journey.

Energies of the Fool

- innocence
- new beginnings
- freedom
- leap of faith
- clear conscious

- trust in self

- the dreamer

- the seed

The Fool's Essential Oil: Peppermint

ELEMENT: Air

PLANETARY INFLUENCE: Mercury

SCENT DESCRIPTION: Peppermint has a very strong and minty scent. The characteristics of the scent are bold, cooling, uplifting, and freeing.

The Fool holds the power of air, spirit, clear consciousness, freedom, and beginnings. He is the dreamer. Air element oils are my clear choice to represent the Fool: peppermint it is! Peppermint brings clarity and thought to the Fool's journey. This oil opens up the mind, helps one breathe freely, and can help support clarity of speech, inspiration, and open thought processes. The air element carries the energy that brings freedom into one's being. It has a linear effect, meaning it can keep one in line, helping to get things done and done correctly. I often work with air oils when I need to accomplish a task because they keep me moving and bring clarity to the project.

To work with peppermint, just carry a bottle of peppermint essential oil with you. Breathe in the stimulating scent three times a day. This is a powerful way to connect to the energy of the Fool. Each time you inhale the scent and think of the Fool, you are calling in air element energies.

Downsides of the Fool

- foolishness

- disregard

- disrespect

- lack of wisdom
- selfish
- indulgent
- materialistic

Tea Recipe for the Fool

DANDELION MINT ICED TEA

For a 2-quart jar, you will need 2 teaspoons of the herb dandelion leaf and 1 teaspoon of the herb peppermint leaf in a tea strainer, then place the strainer in the jar and pour hot water over the tea strainer. Let sit for about 5 to 8 minutes or until it has a golden color. Remove the strainer and allow to cool, then place in the refrigerator. Serve with ice and a pinch of lime if you like. This is a totally uplifting and refreshing tea that also can be served hot.

Support from the Council of Queens

Call in a queen to help support the downside of the Fool. Each queen has a unique property to aid you in your goal.

If the Fool's energy can at times be overwhelming, if you feel as if you have no control or you need grounding during your adventure, then the Queen of Pentacles may be a great companion and guide through this stage of your journey. Creating a grounding essential oil blend to work with will be beneficial at this stage or use a single oil of your choosing—something with an earthy scent. Think of rooting your soul into self and allowing your spirit to fly. The Queen of Pentacles blend is magical and will keep you sure-footed on your journey.

Read through the Queen of Pentacles' message and her journey on page 18, then call in her energy. Ask her to guide you through your Fool's journey as you craft the blend. If you don't wish to use the formula in this book, then choose an earthy oil to work with or create your own blend using earth element oils. Remember to work with peppermint separately for the air elemental energies.

The Queen of Cups can help the Fool show compassion during this exciting time of adventure. One of the downsides to the Fool is the possibility of being overindulgent with disregard and disrespect for others while he is flying high. The Queen of Cups can help open the Fool's heart and make him more aware of those around him. The Queen of Cups can also call in peace, calming, and intuition.

The Fool is on an adventure, and sometimes change and adventure, or stepping into new possibilities, can be a scary situation. The Queen of Wands can help with courage and strength during this time. She can stoke the flames of passion that will encourage embracing the adventure with a desire to move forward and succeed.

Although the Fool is air element, he does not always have his wits about him. The Queen of Swords can help call in logic. She can give the Fool time to breathe and think before stepping too deep in the wrong direction. Call on this queen when the adventure is over-stimulating or when there is a need to stop, breathe, and rest for a moment—to stop and recalculate—before jumping again.

Companion Cards

The Fool's number in the tarot is number 0 and also number 22. The Fool is given the number 22 for numerology purposes, so if you are working with tarot's major arcana through numerology and receive 22, then you get the Fool. This can be reduced further as $2 + 2 = 4$, which is the Emperor. This makes the Emperor the companion card for the Fool.

The two seem like an unlikely pair, yet they need each other. The Fool finds the fatherly support of the Emperor as he jumps off the cliff. Study the Emperor and call in his structure and support. The

Emperor belongs to the fire element, so working with fire elemental oils can give the Fool a much-needed boost. You must remember that air fans fire, and your fire can get out of control if you let the Fool reign. The Emperor is structure, so he can add a container for the burn. This is how these two cards can help each other. You can also create an earthy blend with a bit of spice in it, such as cedarwood and cinnamon or cedarwood and sweet orange. Here you have a grounding effect for the fire of the Emperor.

The Magician

NUMBER: 1

ELEMENT: Earth and air

PLANETARY INFLUENCE: Mercury

A Message from the Magician

I am the Magician, and I resonate within my being the elements of earth and air. I am the spirit manifesting into matter upon the ground. I am always connected to both spirit above and earth below. I have the power to communicate with spirit and Mother Earth at all times; therefore, I have the magical ability of spiritual manifestation upon the earth. I reach up and I point down with my will and intention. This magic comes with the demands of faith in your spirit (above) and belief in self as matter (below).

Meanings

The Magician is numbered one in the major arcana. As number one he stands straight and tall, reaching above and below. In numerology the number one represents the self as well as "the All"—as in we are all one. Even the shape of the number 1 stands straight and tall, reaching up and rooting below, therefore at all times being in tune above with the powers of thought, communication, prayer, and divine connection, as well as below, allowing for manifestation upon the earth.

The Magician has all four elements upon his table as tools ready for use. Air, represented in the tarot as the suit of swords, for communication, truth, inspiration, connecting with source, and clarity. The element of fire, represented in the tarot as the suit of wands, for courage, strength, charisma, creativity, transformation, and the will to become. The element of water, represented in the tarot as the suit of cups, inspires movement, compassion, the inner voice, intuition, emotional strength, and internal wisdom; the mysteries within. Last but not least, the gift of the earth element, represented in the tarot as the suit of pentacles, to manifest upon and create your best self.

The Magician asks you to believe in yourself and create the human being you wish to be. Without a belief in himself and the divine, the Magician does not have the faith to create and manifest with abundance. I have a friend who has the Magician as her soul card. We met for lunch one day and she showed me some of her creations. She makes gorgeous tarot bags, tarot cloths, and larger messenger bags. At the time she did not believe her work was valuable. She did not think she would be able to sell her work. I convinced her to look at what she was creating in a different manner. Her work was beautiful and valuable. I bought some of her work on the spot and encouraged her to get a booth at the Northwest Tarot Symposium (NWTS), a yearly event in the Portland, Oregon, area. She did, and she sold out of her products on the first day of the event. That night she went home and created more to sell. This happened six years ago. Today her magical bags are sold in many stores. The key lies in believing in yourself.

The Magician asks you to step up, believe in your abilities, and take the next step. Remember: you are the Magician, with the power to create. You have all you need on your table. Now is the time to believe in yourself.

Energies of the Magician

- manifestation
- power
- confidence
- communication

- timing
- magic
- belief in self and the all
- flexibility
- will and focused intention to become

The Magician's Essential Oil: Virginia cedarwood
ELEMENT: Earth, fire, water, air
PLANETARY INFLUENCE: Jupiter, Mercury
SCENT DESCRIPTION: Woody, sweet, mellow, deep, and earthy

Cedarwood oil is extracted by steam distillation from the wood of the tree. Virginia cedarwood is the oil I recommend because cedarwood Atlas is on the endangered species list. I find Virginia cedarwood has a soft, woody scent and is a wonderful addition to a blend or used as inhalant all by itself.

I chose cedarwood to embrace the energy of the Magician for several reasons. In my opinion, cedarwood relates to all four of the four elemental energies—perfect for our Magician. Cedarwood's purifying quality is often used to purify and cleanse. It is also beneficial when working with elemental magic. Cedarwood relates to the water element in its ability to increase intuition—opening the upper energy channels for vision, dream work, and calling in one's psychic abilities.

Cedar carries an earthy, beautiful scent. When I smell cedarwood, I am immediately taken to a forest where I'm supported, grounded, and nurtured. Since cedarwood is distilled from the wood of the tree, this adds to the solidity and grounding energies of this oil as well as provides a balanced energy for the Magician. Cedarwood is also associated with money and abundance; hence, it contains the element of earth. Cedarwood embraces the fire element with its powerful energies for creating magic and its purification qualities. Cedarwood is often burned for purification purposes. It brings the energy of courage and strength. Cedar is great for banishing. Think of how we often use cedar's banishing power to keep away fleas and insects in pet beds. We also place important treasures in cedar chests as cedarwood keeps these treasures safe from pests and the outside environment, therefore calling in the energy of protection. The air element comes in because cedar, like sage, has been burned for centuries. North American Indigenous Nations used cedar to help enhance communication with their ancestors and guides, as well as for purification and sending prayers up to the heavens.

Cedarwood blends well with citrus oils, other woody oils, and floral, spicy, or herbaceous oils. I suggest you create a blend that carries earth and air element qualities for the Magician. It depends on how you want to use the blend. Add a fire oil to the blend if you want the Magician's power of magic. Use an air element blend for communication. Think of which characteristics of the Magician you need right now and amp up that element in your blend.

CEDARWOOD CLEANSING STICK

Gather cedar and bind together with rope or string. Allow it to dry before burning it. The scent is so beautiful and magical. You can add some lavender to your bundle if you wish. Burn this bundle daily for as long as it lasts in honor of the Magician.

Downsides of the Magician

- ego
- untapped potential
- destruction
- lack of will to become
- lack of belief in self

Support from the Council of Queens

Call in a queen to help support a downside of the Magician. Each queen has a unique property to aid you in your goal. Any of the queens could be of assistance since the Magician has all four elemental tools upon his table. Use the Queen of Pentacles to add growth, abundance, and grounding to the table, as well as a solid belief in self. Use the Queen of Cups for self-trust, intuition, dream work, psychic abilities, and flow. Use the Queen of Wands for magic, courage, will, desire, and creativity. Finally, use the Queen of Swords for communication, clarity, and speaking your truth.

Companion Cards

The Magician is number 1 in the tarot. Since there are twenty-two major arcana cards, we can look at what other cards reduce down to the number one: 19 and 10. We have two potential companion cards to work with here. The Sun (19) can support freedom, success, and the ability to shine. Work with the Sun when you want to be seen or when you are required to lead. Call in charisma, and allow yourself to shine for others to see. The Sun will support outward expansion and success.

The Wheel of Fortune (10) helps us access change and the power of going with the flow. You can call in the energy of the Wheel of Fortune to help manifest the changes you wish to create in your life. Make a list of all you wish to manifest and then do the work.

The High Priestess

NUMBER: 2

ELEMENT: Water

PLANETARY INFLUENCE: Moon

A Message from the High Priestess

You are here because you don't trust yourself yet. You are fearful of this journey. Do you believe you deserve this journey? You are ready; you really are. You have made it this far and know what you must do. You have been following the path your whole life and are at a crossroads. You have chosen your path. In fact, you have already taken a few steps in your chosen direction. You are being led by the golden thread. Follow it because this is where you wish to be. Know this.

Meanings

The High Priestess carries the energies of duality, choice, yin and yang, relationship, intuition, and internal knowing. We have choices to make and relationships to form. With the energy of the Magician being self-manifestation, the High Priestess calls in balance, duality, choice, and relationship with the number 2. The High Priestess asks you to listen to your internal knowing, your truth. She has a constant connection with the unconscious, the divine, and the deep well of knowledge that lives within. The High Priestess trusts her intuition and looks deep into her well of knowledge. She knows when to be quiet, when to speak, when to be still, and when to allow the flow of water to create movement to the outer world.

If the High Priestess has entered your life or you are calling on the High Priestess for guidance, you are being asked to be still and listen to your truth. What does your intuition tell you? What are the secrets, mysteries, and answers that lie within? The High Priestess allows for meditation, ritual, water, effortless flow, silence, peace, secrets, and wisdom. It is now time to wait, listen, trust, and observe. The answer lies within.

The High Priestess helps you become still in order to go within and find truth and listen to your internal knowing. Trust your gut. This is not the time to speak. Gather the necessary information from within. Listen, be silent, and wait. Learn to accept stillness. All of the answers to your greatest questions lie within yourself. Listen and you will know.

Energies of the High Priestess

- wisdom
- knowing
- intuition
- stillness
- peace
- duality
- relationship

The High Priestess's Essential Oil: Clary Sage

ELEMENT: Earth, air, water

PLANETARY INFLUENCE: Moon, Mercury

SCENT DESCRIPTION: Clary sage has a deep herbaceous scent with almost a thickness or richness to it. The oil emits a musk, giving it a deep, warm aroma. There is an openness to the scent that pulls one deep into the soul.

I chose clary sage because of its planetary influence of the Moon. I can feel the mysterious, soft energies of this oil. Even though clary sage is often classified as belonging to the element of earth, there is a flowing energy that lives within clary sage's being. The leaf of the clary sage plant is covered with silvery hair. This is an indication of the lunar energy within the plant. Clary sage's Latin name is *Salvia sclarea*. Many members of the Salvia family have these silver hairs on their leaves; thus, they all hold moon energy. The word *clary* relates to the word "clear" and the second half of the name, *sclarea*, relates to the eyes. One possible translation is "clear vision." Think of this vision as "moon vision," or seeing in the dark, representing one's intuition. Therefore, clary sage enhances one's psychic abilities, intuition, self-trust, knowing, and wisdom.

Clary sage is a nervine. A nervine helps to calm the nervous system, therefore having a relaxing effect on the body. It is a sedative and has a calming and mildly intoxicating effect. Used medicinally, clary sage helps with different emotional states such as depression and anxiety. Yet it has an uplifting effect, sometimes promoting a state of euphoria. This calming energy is a powerful ally for meditation, dream work, and opening the mind for night vision. Carry clary sage with you if you need to trust your gut or gather knowledge from your third eye. It helps with any type of psychic or dream work.

Clary sage is a herbaceous essential oil. It can be added as a middle note to your blends and blends well with woody or fruity oils. Add another water element oil to your blend to bring out its feminine, intuitive side. Add a fruity oil scent to expand on the euphoria. This will make an uplifting blend. You can also mix clary sage with air oils to receive inspirational messages from above.

INCENSE
Burn a clary sage incense to reach the ancestors.

DIFFUSE
Diffuse clary sage essential oil along with some Roman chamomile essential oil to relax and meditate with. Allow yourself to reach your inner High Priestess.

Downsides of the High Priestess

- illusion

- secrets

- deceit

- using one's knowing to deceive

Support from the Council of Queens

If you wish to increase the aspects of night vision, intuition, and psychic abilities, call in the Queen of Cups to assist your work. The more Water elemental energies you bring in, the more you connect with the dark, the mysteries, and the deep within. I think of the combination of the High Priestess and the Queen of Cups as a double whammy of feminine knowing and wisdom.

Call in the Queen of Swords for clarity, inspiration, and practical wisdom; especially if illusion or delusion has set in. She will help cut through the muck and make things clear.

Call in the Queen of Pentacles to lay a solid ground for the flow of the High Priestess's watery ways. Being grounded can help with the downside of illusion and deceit. The water element can cause one to tend to live in a dream world or a world of illusion. When working with the energy of the High Priestess, it could be easy to fall into this world of illusion, which in turn can create fear. Fear is counterproductive to trusting your intuition. Standing on solid ground allows for self-trust, making the positive energy of the High Priestess more accessible.

Call in the Queen of Wands to support courage for the High Priestess—the courage to trust her intuition and the courage to use the knowledge she holds within. Although fire and water do not mix, there can be a warming effect here for the High Priestess's cool water. This can open up the High Priestess, allowing her to be more aware of her passion and desire (fire element), which can lead to stepping forward with her inner knowing rather than just sitting in it.

Companion Cards

The High Priestess is number 2 in the tarot. Which major arcana cards reduce down to the number 2? Justice (11: $1 + 1 = 2$) and Judgment (20: $2 + 0 = 2$). Calling on either one of these energies for support is an option. If you remember how the High Priestess carries the energy of duality and choice, you can see how Justice can help create balance. The High Priestess helps us tap into our intuition, while Justice helps us bring clarity and a masculine energy to the flow, allowing us to use our intuition and create reality. Judgment can help us take a deep look at what needs to be shifted in our lives to bring about rebirth. Tapping into our intuition and diving deep into our cave allows us to emerge anew. Choose to work with Judgment when you want to use your intuition to hear the call or see the big picture for possible rebirth.

The Empress

NUMBER: 3

ELEMENT: Earth

PLANETARY INFLUENCE: Venus

A Message from the Empress

Everything I touch expands and grows. Like vines that crawl upon the ground, reaching for required nourishment and new horizons, I will nourish you. I bring opportunity, advancement, and forward movement. I am the Mother. I will care for you, guide you, and allow you to flourish. Sit upon my throne and allow the earth to surround you and bring you comfort. You are loved. You can now move forward with abundance. Look at what surrounds you; take in the messages of the mother. Allow yourself to grow and create. Be open to receive and be ready to dig your hands in the nurturing dirt. Dig deep. I offer myself to you. Be grateful for all you have been given. You have all you need to flourish.

Meanings

If you have chosen to work with the Empress or the Empress has chosen you, then you are in a place of abundance, growth, fertility, and nurturing energy. The question is are you the nurturer or are you open to receive? Maybe both answers are true. Give and take creates a balanced energy. The Empress is like Mother Nature. She gives and she is open to receive the bounty of the earth. Now is the time to grow, accept what is being given, and push forward. The Empress offers creative energy allowing one to accomplish and create new ground to move upon.

Remember that the number for the Fool is 0, meaning the seed, new beginnings, and freedom. Then we look at the Magician, whose number is 1 and is about self-manifestation. The number 2 of the High Priestess brings in duality, choice, relationship, wisdom, and self-knowledge. The number 3, the Empress, brings in growth from combining 1 and 2 together. Now we are given the opportunity to grow our creative manifestation that started with the Magician and the seeds of the Fool.

The Empress offers a positive energy to all creative endeavors. She is beauty in the form of mother, creator, fertile ground, offspring, growth, abundance, the earth. The Empress is like creative growth ready to burst free. Alejandro Jodorowsky, in his book *The Way of Tarot: The Spiritual Teacher in the Cards*, calls the Empress "a Creative Outburst, Expression." This is a period of growth; the cycle of creativity.

Often those folks with Empress energy become herbalists, veterinarians, social workers, nurses, gardeners, and mothers. These individuals take care of and nurture others into growth.

The seeds you planted are flourishing now. Nourish them, water them, feed them, love them, and you will find you are embraced in the arms of the Mother. It is time to take care of yourself and your creative being. The Empress can also offer help with illness and health issues by teaching us how to nurture ourselves as she gives healing energy. The message here is to take care of your body and allow yourself to heal. Be as the vine upon the ground: reaching and growing. You hold the seed of abundance in your hands. Plant it and watch it grow. These are the gifts of the Empress.

When I calculated my personal year numerology back to my birth, I was most surprised that in my one and only Empress year, believe it or not, I was pregnant with my daughter and she was born in my Empress year. How cool is that?

Energies of the Empress

- growth
- abundance
- fertility
- creativity
- marriage
- nurture
- comfort
- beauty
- maternal energy
- lust

The Empress's Essential Oil: Patchouli

ELEMENT: Earth

PLANETARY INFLUENCE: Saturn

SCENT DESCRIPTION: Patchouli is a rich, thick scent, earthy and empowering. Patchouli is warm, deep, and sensual. There is a wildness about it, catering to a sense of freedom. There is a sensuality and feminine energy that expands the sense of beauty and rawness. The scent of patchouli reminds me of steak sauce and makes me hungry for meat. This calls in the wild of the hunt. Wearing patchouli sets one free with a deep sense of rootedness.

I tried really hard not to choose patchouli for the Empress. The more research I conducted, the more I realized how fitting patchouli was. Patchouli just seemed like the logical choice, and I wanted something unique. The essential oil kept speaking to me, and I had to agree with her. She is the Empress. The deep, earthy scent vitalizes the senses and calls in lust, fertility, and love. It allows the wild animal instincts of the earth to infuse our body and mind with passion. Patchouli is an aphrodisiac, which also ties into the energy of raw wildness.

Patchouli carries the gifts of abundance, prosperity, and money, allowing for financial healthiness and growth. Like the Empress, patchouli provides for the sense of a deep rootedness in self. This creates a grounded trust of one's abilities and helps one create boundaries as well as new growth patterns.

Patchouli is a scent of freedom, beauty, raw earthy lust, warmth, comfort, abundance, and fertility. Wearing patchouli not only helps to ground oneself; it helps make one feel beautiful.

Patchouli brings happiness, dance, joy, freedom, and peace, which is why it's known as "the hippy oil." Use patchouli by diffusing or creating a grounding spray for a happy, peaceful home.

Starting off a blend with patchouli as a grounding base note is the way to go. Add higher note essential oils on top of it. I recommend the other earthy, woody oils. They'll blend beautifully with patchouli. Also try the herbaceous, spicy, and floral oils. I love my Queen of Pentacles blend (see recipe on page 22) for the deep and earthy tones she carries. You can use this blend for the Empress as well.

Downsides of the Empress

- stubborn
- set in her ways
- overcautious
- smothering
- lack of boundaries

Support from the Council of Queens

Call in a queen to help support a downside of the Empress card. Each queen has a unique property to aid you in your goal. Choose to work with the Queen of Wands to call in your magic. She can help you create, empower, and call in your strength and courage for your adventure. She will also help with leadership and charisma.

Call in the Queen of Cups for health and healing when working with the Empress. Water adds a bit of movement if the Empress energy is rooted too deep and one needs to bring in flow.

The Queen of Swords adds some direction for the force of creative energy abounding from the Empress. Air energy helps connect the energy of abundance with the energy of directed force to create the appropriate outcome for one's desires.

Since both the Empress and the Queen of Pentacles are earth element, you can work with Queen of Pentacles energies to reinforce qualities of the Empress that you wish to bring to the forefront. For example, if health is an issue and you are working with the Empress to support a healthy lifestyle, then the Queen of Pentacles can create the healthy garden or support a grounded choice to stay away from sugar. Use the Queen of Pentacles' stubborn side to dig your heels into the dirt and not allow yourself to stray. Ask the Queen of Pentacles to lay a solid foundation for the growth that the Empress will bring into your life. The Queen of Pentacles can create structure for the growth and abundance you are calling into your life with the energy of the Empress.

Companion Cards

The Empress is number 3 in the tarot. Companion cards are the Hanged Man (12) and the World (21). The Hanged Man is $1 + 2 = 3$ and the World is $2 + 1 = 3$. Call upon either of these cards for support. The Hanged Man will ask you to look at things from a different perspective and to let go and surrender. The earth element energy can be stubborn and tends to hold on to things and not let go. The Hanged Man will assist in letting go of what needs to be released so that a new way forward can be found. The World card is success. This is the energy we all wish to live in. We have made it to a certain point in our life. The Empress, being growth and abundance, is striving to reach the World, and in this numerology we see that success can be accomplished. Work with the World card to envision and move toward the whole. The World can also help to set up boundaries and release self-limiting beliefs.

The Emperor

NUMBER: 4

ELEMENT: Fire

ASTROLOGICAL INFLUENCE: Aries

A Message from the Emperor

I am the Emperor. I am fire, courage, control. As the Empress is the Mother, I am the Father. I have an open, caring heart, but I can be overbearing and controlling at times. I will listen and guide. I inform and demand. I am those in control, the government and authority, but I am also you in your own internal paternal self. I am here to help you create your kingdom. I am on your side. With the Empress you gained growth and abundance. With me, the Emperor, you gain structure, security, passion, and authority. I will help you put things in place. As you have grown, now you will build.

Meanings

If you have chosen the Emperor or if the Emperor has chosen you, it is a time to take back your life. This is a card about leadership, gaining control, taking charge, and owning it. Now is the time to be responsible for yourself and care for those around you. You are full of fire and charisma. Others wish to listen and follow. Create, build, and be responsible for your work. The Emperor could represent a time to reach out to an authority figure for help. Get in touch with your father or a governmental body or talk to an expert in a field of your choice.

When I need guidance from the Emperor, I pull the Emperor card and do a reading around it. Put the Emperor down in front of you. Shuffle your deck, pull four other cards, and place them around the Emperor: one placed above and one below, one to the right and one to the left. These cards advise you on which elemental energies are asking for guidance. Interpret the spread according to the elemental composition. If swords (air) surround the Emperor, seek guidance in the field of communication—possibly publishers or editors. Or it's time to step on the stage and communicate your passion. If you see more pentacles (earth), then seek out financial advice. Wands (fire) may be telling you to get creative—advertising, marketing, acting, or creating magic. Finally, cups (water) represent the need for emotional or relationship focus—counseling or spiritual input. If you associate the suit of cups with intuition, the appearance of cups surrounding the Emperor may be indicating the need to follow your intuitive hunches.

If you are the Emperor in the above reading, then these four cards surrounding you are the areas in which you need to put your focus on at this time—the message being "Here is where you need to start."

In his book *The Life You Were Born to Live: A Guide to Finding Your Life Purpose*, Dan Millman correlates the number 4 to the power of stability and process. This means that for the Emperor, the process of getting to the fruition of a project is just as important as setting the foundation and the journey that leads you to fruition. Integrity, flexibility, honesty, and grounded movement forward are all necessary for the Emperor to be a success.

The Emperor carries the energy of fire, power, will, focused intention, authority, strength, courage, and charisma. Carry these powers with grace and compassion. Remember the stories of the emperor who wore no clothes and King Midas. You may have power and control, but be careful of what you wish for. You may need to set up boundaries and create order, but do so with an open heart. You are in control, but sometimes those in control can lead others astray. Honesty and integrity are important characteristics at this time. Stand tall, be strong, and lead.

Energies of the Emperor

- control

- power

- courage

- boundaries

- charisma

- paternal figure

- masculine

- fire

- structure

- leadership

- protection

- success

The Emperor's Essential Oil: Oakwood Absolute

ELEMENT: Earth, fire

PLANETARY INFLUENCE: Mars

SCENT DESCRIPTION: Oakwood absolute has a
deep, earthy, woody scent with a hint of vanilla and
rum. This magical scent takes you deep into the
forest. The quality of the oil is thick and heavy, yet
this beautiful scent creates a vitality and strength as
well as a warmth about it.

I love the energy of the great oak tree, which stands tall and
strong. The oak is a symbol of strength, courage, protection, knowledge, wisdom, and honor. The oak grows slowly but has a foundation that grows strong, giving the oak the ability to last for hundreds
of years. Greek mythology associates the oak with Thor, the god of
thunder. This is interesting because the oak tends to stand taller than
other trees and often holds more moisture. Because of this, the oak

has a strong electrical conductivity, making it more susceptible to being struck by lightning. I feel this association to Thor is the gift of the god to the mighty oak. It is a warning system put in place by Thor that lightning is on the way.

Oak also teaches us about flexibility. An oak doesn't bend like the willow, so it tends to break under the power of wind. This is a lesson for the Emperor as well. At times the Emperor can become so entrenched in his own ego or having the order of control that he tends not to bend to what may be needed to accomplish his goal. He is not willing to bend to the wisdom or lesson of the time. The mighty oak can help to enforce this lesson of flexibility.

One more aspect that I personally feel is an important contribution of the oak tree is the acorn. The acorn is a seed and therefore represents the fire element, the desire and will to become, the spark. The acorn is a strong and powerful symbol of the Emperor as the acorn starts as the seed that forms the foundation for growth and creates the strong, powerful, mighty oak. The acorn creates form and structure, as does the Emperor.

Oakwood absolute is a very deep, earthy scent that is grounding and powerful. The scent will take you deep into the forest and your bones, creating a secure, protected, open ground to build upon. Use oakwood absolute as your base note and build upon it. This oil is a woody oil that blends well with spicy, floral, herbaceous, and other woody scents. I believe a little bit of citrus is nice also.

Downsides of the Emperor

- egotistical
- lack of flexibility
- overly controlling
- demanding
- unable to see through others' eyes

- overprotective
- dictator

Support from the Council of Queens

Aggressive behavior is a sign of an overabundance of Emperor energy. Call in the Queen of Cups to open the emotional energies and to put out some of the fire. She is so interconnected to water that she can help open up the heart and infuse it with more compassion. We know the Emperor has heart—he is a father figure—but he may need to be reminded of his emotions on occasion. The Queen of Cups can also help the Emperor to tap into the third eye of intuition, giving him the ability to see a clear path to move forward.

The Queen of Pentacles helps the Emperor down from his high horse and get deep into his bones to see what truly is rather than what his ego is telling him. She can ground the Emperor and create a safe place for his fire to burn. Setting up boundaries that will allow the fire to remain contained yet burn to its greatest heights allows the flames to be directed with focused intention. This will create a more solid outcome with no additional out of control fires to put out.

The Queen of Swords can assist the Emperor with focus and order, but remember that the air element can fan the flames of fire even higher, so beware not to let the ego and fear into your thought processes.

Although the Emperor and the Queen of Wands are both fire element, calling in the energies of the Queen of Wands can be of great support to the Emperor. The Emperor carries that masculine energy—he is the father figure but sometimes he will need to dip into his feminine side. He can do this with the Queen of Wands. She can teach him magic and the power of the cauldron. The Queen of Wands will teach the Emperor how to use his magic to create his world. She can teach him to use his charisma and passion with a less dominant tone, therefore opening the doors to a better reception from his followers.

Companion Cards

The Emperor is number 4 in the tarot. His companion card is the Fool because adding 22 together gets us 4 in 2 + 2 = 4. Remember that the Fool is given the number 22 for numerology purposes. Calling upon support from the Fool may be an option. If you think of the Emperor, you may think of structure, security, leadership, and a fatherly nature. At times there is a need for some "foolish" energy. The Emperor needs to be able to let go and embrace some freedom for his own good as well as the good of those who follow him. He also needs to be able to take the leap of faith when needed. He needs to be able to sometimes embrace risk and not be fearful of movement forward. The Fool can be his guide to be open to fun and bring in the sense of freedom as well as call in the energy of the dreamer and the risk taker.

The Hierophant

NUMBER: 5

ELEMENT: Earth

ASTROLOGICAL INFLUENCE: Taurus

A Message from the Hierophant

I am the Hierophant, the companion and partner to the High Priestess. The High Priestess represents the feminine/ moon energy and I the masculine/sun energy, although I carry the energy of the earth. I can represent many things. I am the higher echelon of society in the form of higher education and the world's religions and churches. I help one conform to society and fit in, yet I am the revealer and channeler of mysteries. I am spirituality, the search for meaning, and I am the channel in that I translate wisdom for the masses. I am tradition in that I have walked many paths. I am the wise counsel that you seek; the question is, do you wish to conform to my doctrines? Do you wish to be a part of it? Listen as I speak, for I am wisdom in many forms.

Meanings

If you are working with the Hierophant, it may be time to seek counsel. There are many forms of counsel. Gaining knowledge in the form of higher education and learning is one way. Connecting to spirituality by joining a church or seeking personal connection through a spiritual system is another. Perhaps you are the Hierophant, channeling messages for others, translating knowledge that may be difficult or foreign. I went back to school in a recent Hierophant year. I enrolled in a nine-month herbalist certification course, conforming to new rules and structure. I gained so much new knowledge.

The Hierophant represents spirituality, tradition, teaching, and learning. He is both translator and channel. The Hierophant belongs to the earth element. He represents what happens in this world. Dan Millman calls the number five "the energy of freedom and discipline." Through disciplined structure comes the freedom to create your true desires in reality.

As a young girl, I searched and searched for spirituality, as well as form and structure—a religion to give me support and faith. Yes, I was totally into tarot and magic, yet at the same time I searched for my roots through church. My family is from the deep hills of Kentucky. As churchgoers, they ranged from Pentecostal to Baptist.

My grandfather, William Farmer Shepherd, was known as Preacher Willie. In addition to being a preacher, he was also a coal miner. He died of black lung before I was born. On my mother's side of the family, we had Grandpa Will Begley. He was a gun-toting bootlegger. By the time I knew Grandpa Will, he was no longer a bootlegger. He had gotten sober. Grandmother Edna, Will's wife, was an herbalist. I often heard my mother speak of some concoction that her mother had made. Usually secondhand, like "Mommy would make a liniment for that."

So the spirit of religion and the spirit of a cunning woman both grew within me. I went to many different churches—Jehovah's Witnesses, Catholic, Baptist, Methodist, and Pentecostal—with no avail. At times I felt the spirit touch me within, but I never quite fit in and I never could take in all their beliefs.

I saw myself as an eternal seeker looking for a place to fit in, a place to bring me discipline, a physical structure. I found that discipline and structure within by finding my own spirituality. Sometimes discipline can carry new knowledge that opens new doors and eventually offers a newfound freedom. At other times we need to conform to fit into a place or circumstance just for a while until we have the knowledge to move out on our own. I had difficulty trying to conform to all the spiritual belief systems of the churches I attended. The Hierophant is asking you to either seek wisdom through learning or spirituality or to become the Hierophant and channel wisdom to others. If seeking wisdom from another, you will need to conform in some way to the doctrines of their beliefs.

Energies of the Hierophant

- tradition
- spirituality
- wisdom
- knowledge
- conformity
- discipline
- change
- channel
- revealer of mysteries

The Hierophant's Essential Oil: Frankincense

ELEMENT: Fire, water

PLANETARY INFLUENCE: Moon, sun

SCENT DESCRIPTION: Frankincense essential oil is earthy and woody yet at the same time offers a lightness about it with a hint of sweetness.

Frankincense comes from the oleo-gum resin of a small shrub with pinnate leaves and white or pink flowers. This oleo-resin is steam-distilled and processed into frankincense essential oil. Oleo-resins, gums, and saps form on the tree trunk as a healing agent for the tree. Therefore, these types of gums and resins are often considered healers. Frankincense has been used as a sacred scent for many moons.

The oil is very thick, and it can get so thick that it becomes unusable. If this happens, use hot water (by soaking or running hot tap water over the bottle) to melt the resin into a liquid state again.

Frankincense is very calming. It has a deep and peaceful scent that is great for meditation, and it helps reduce stress. It was one of the sacred gifts given by the Three Wise Men to Jesus upon his birth, and it was used by the Egyptians as offerings to the gods. Frankincense incense has been used in sacred ceremonies to connect with the divine. According to Sandra Kynes in her marvelous book *Mixing Essential Oils for Magic: Aromatic Alchemy for Personal Blends*, frankincense has a long tradition and magical connection with spirituality. Frankincense calls in the energies of inspiration and knowledge and helps with all things spiritual. It is helpful for dream work, psychic work, and divination. Since frankincense is a resin, it blends well with other resinous oils like myrrh and with floral and spicy scent groups. Use frankincense as a base note, then build upon it.

People burn the resin as an incense, using charcoal as a burning base. Make a ritual out of burning the incense by offering the scent and rising smoke as a gift to your guides every morning. This helps open the channel between spirit and matter.

Downsides of the Hierophant

- rebellion
- rejection of doctrines or values
- unsound advice

Support from the Council of Queens

Call in a queen to help support a downside of the Hierophant. Each queen has a unique property to aid you in your goal. Since the Hierophant is the earth element, with the capability to channel the divine, I would call in the Queen of Cups. She can help boost the desire to work with the mysteries, intuition, psychic abilities, channeling, or any form of spirituality. She can also boost any form of healing, internal or external.

For inspiration, knowledge, schoolwork, and wisdom, call in the Queen of Swords. She will not only bring you clarity, she will get you focused so you can do whatever work needs to be completed. The Queen of Swords will keep you in line so that knowledge can be gained for proper use.

The Queen of Wands can help connect with your inner spark, your spirit, as well as create ritual for divine connection.

The Queen of Pentacles can help keep the Hierophant grounded. Rebellion, rejection of doctrine or values, and unsound advice are the downfall of the Hierophant. We have seen spiritual leaders lose their grounding many times in our society. Having the Queen of Pentacles as a guide for the Hierophant can make him really call in the positive earthy qualities that he may require, such as being trustworthy, the salt of the earth. This can help him give solid and grounded advice. If the Hierophant is struggling with doing what he feels is the best thing he can do, he may need to take a really grounded approach to the matter at hand.

Companion Cards

The Hierophant is number 5 in the tarot. The other card that reduces down to 5 is Temperance, number 14: $1 + 4 = 5$. Temperance can keep the Hierophant from going to extremes. Temperance speaks of the middle way, of staying in balance internally, and of internal healing. I feel that Temperance can help the Hierophant to see the whole yet walk in the middle, allowing for compassion, vision, and support of spirit. With Temperance we are combining and merging, allowing for healing and creating a new blend of you; a new harmony, so to speak. The Hierophant asks you to merge with your spirituality, your higher development and tradition, as well as to conform and fit in. Temperance will help you be you yet also blend, conform, and create a cooperation with the energies of the Hierophant.

The Lovers

NUMBER: 6

ELEMENT: Air

ASTROLOGICAL INFLUENCE: Gemini

A Message from the Lovers

You will hold many hands in this lifetime. If you could imagine all the people you have met in your life and imagine that you are holding their hand, you would see an infinite line of soul personalities. You have been in a relationship of some sort with all of these individuals at one time. As you move through your life, you will let go of many hands and you will open your hand to accept new ones. The Lovers card represents a shifting of a relationship or multiple relationships. There are decisions to be made. You are at a crossroads, and I offer you the power of choice.

Meanings

If you have chosen the Lovers or the Lovers has chosen you, you are (or will be) experiencing changes in the relationships of your life. Are you in a love relationship that is changing—marriage or new love? Is there another shift happening? Are you leaving something behind or is something leaving you behind? Whatever this change is, it will create a new balance in your life. The Lovers card is numbered 6, which creates new balance (3 + 3). During this time you can let go of relationships and call in new ones to create new beginnings. Maybe you take a relationship you are currently in to a new dimension. There will be choices to make as you stand at the crossroads of life.

The Lovers is an interesting card to work with. Many people think this card indicates a love relationship or marriage. While the Lovers can and does speak about love and marriage, I often find this card means something different. It all depends on what is being asked. The Lovers card also speaks of choices to be made, and these choices will often influence the loss and creation of relationships.

I am a true believer in the numerology of one's personal year. I'm currently in my Lovers year as I write this. I have watched several friends as well as my husband in their Lovers year to see what happens. Here is what I have personally seen. In the case of my husband, he ended up quitting his job and taking a few months off to reevaluate. During this time off, he started playing his guitar again, started jamming with others, and became part of a new musical community. He had been very unhappy at his job and decided he had had enough. Through this decision came a shifting of relationships. Out with the old work relationships and in with the new music community. He found a new job during his following year, which was a Chariot year for him.

I am currently in my Lovers year, and within three weeks of my birthday and movement into my Lovers year, I was laid off from my job due to the COVID-19 pandemic. I currently sit here with no job but a grand opportunity to write this book. I do not feel like I will go back to my job. I believe some new relationship is forming in the line of my work. This shifting of relationships so far has led me in a new direction with a new possible writing community through editing, publishing, and the many writers I am connecting with at this time. I did not physically make this decision to leave my job—it was made for me—but the timing was grand. I am learning to let go of what I cannot control and accept that there are new hands offering themselves to me for continued growth. In *The Way of Tarot: The Spiritual Teacher in the Cards*, Alejandro Jodorowsky speaks of the Lovers card as a card of union and disunion—a shifting of outside social choices as well as internal emotional choices. I call it a shifting in relationship or relationships. What is changing in your world of relationships right now?

Energies of the Lovers

- love
- marriage
- relationship
- union
- disunion
- choice
- shifting of relationship energies

The Lovers Essential Oil: Lavender

ELEMENT: Air

PLANETARY INFLUENCE: Mercury

SCENT DESCRIPTION: Lavender is an extremely popular scent and has been for centuries. Lavender is light and airy with a sharpness to it; it is flowery yet not overly sweet. A deep breath of lavender is clearing in thought and opens the air passages as well as the third eye.

I chose lavender for a couple of reasons. Number one, lavender is an air element oil gathered from the leaves and flowers of the plant. The Lovers card carries the energy of air as well. Lavender is an emotional balancer in that it is calming to emotional states. Lavender has been used for centuries by many communities as an attractant as well as a repellent. According to Amy Blackthorn in her book *Botanical Magic: The Green Witch's Guide to Essential Oils for Spellcraft, Ritual and Healing*, the work of the Victorian Flower Oracle states that lavender's language is that of being devoted to another. Lavender speaks of attraction. Women of the night would often wear lavender to attract men as well as to protect themselves from the possible violence from those they attracted. As one travels through the Lovers card, one can use lavender to help with emotional states, bring clarity of thought for choices to be made, as well as call in inspiration and attract what is needed at the time: whether it be a partner or sought-after energies or individuals for a project or spell. Lavender attracts and lavender protects. During the time of the plague, the town of Bucklersbury, England, was spared of the illness due to the fact that they were in the center of the European lavender industry. All were spared; all remained healthy. In this way lavender can protect not only from illness but from unwanted energies, attention, and violence. It is all in one's intention for the oil.

When I first entered into my Lovers year this last March, I was all of a sudden totally attracted to lavender. I would wear it at night, at bedtime, or to make me feel beautiful and peaceful during the day. I also have about eight lavender plants growing in my small garden, and the urge to make a lovely lavender oil infusion as well as a hydrosol has been speaking to me.

Lavender is a middle note and blends well with other flowers as well as woody, herbaceous, and citrus oils. Lavender is one of the safest oils for use and at times can be used neat, meaning by itself with no carrier oil. I always recommend carriers if possible but in a pinch a drop of lavender will not harm.

Again, lavender is calming and helps with anxiety and depression. Lavender attracts as all flowers do, but lavender is also a protector and can banish unwanted energies and help fight off illness. Lavender can bring clarity and inspiration, therefore helping you make decisions with open eyes. As one moves through the energy of the Lovers, working with the sweet energy of lavender can help bring a peaceful and clear journey.

LAVENDER TEA

You can add a few lavender flowers to an herbal tea such as chamomile. Both lavender and chamomile are calming and will help you relax and call in restful sleep. Lavender is strong, so don't use too much.

LAVENDER SALT BATH

Add about 8–10 drops of lavender essential oil to 1 tablespoon jojoba oil and add to bath. Then take 1 cup of Epsom or Dead Sea salts (or ½ cup of each) and pour into running bath water. Relax to bring clarity to the mind and clear the aura.

Downsides of the Lovers

- indecision
- separation
- manipulation
- temptation

Support from the Council of Queens

We are already in the air element here with the Lovers card, so calling in the Queen of Swords would always be okay. She will just reinforce the air element qualities needed to move forward on the path. The only thing about the Queen of Swords is that she is the least emotional queen in the bunch. She will help make decisions with a clear head. Emotions are not her thing. In order to really work with the emotional energies of this card, call in the Queen of Cups. Of course, if you are too much up in the air and this relationship (or relationships) is taking over your ability to think clearly and make the right decisions, then asking advice from the Queen of Pentacles for grounding may be the way to go. For feet firmly planted while one's head is in the clouds, the Queen of Pentacles will make for solid footing through this journey. If you need to stoke the fires of passion in a relationship, then call in the Queen of Wands to stir the pot a bit and get the flames going again.

Companion Card

The Lovers is number 6 in the tarot. The companion card would be number 15, the Devil: $1 + 5 = 6$. The Devil may be an option for support with the Lovers. The Devil card can help bring unhealthy attachments into focus. In this manner, the Devil can help release attachments that are keeping you bound to unfortunate addictions, relationships, or fears. The Devil also tells you to have some fun and be a little devilish, helping spice up current relationships.

The Chariot

NUMBER: 7

ELEMENT: Water

ASTROLOGICAL INFLUENCE: Cancer

A Message from the Chariot

I am the Chariot. I give you the gift of movement forward. It is time to gather your courage and go for it. What is it that is ready to be born in the world? What is it you are driving toward? I will help you move forward, toward your destiny, and I will help you succeed. The key is that you must stay focused. You must have willpower and the desire for victory. I am water, so emotions will be involved. As you travel the road, it is okay to feel your emotions, but don't react or you will scare the horses and they will lose their way. You will lose your way. Use your protective shield to soothe your emotions as you travel toward victory.

Meanings

If you have chosen the Chariot or the Chariot has chosen you, it is a time of forward movement. You have a powerful and exciting journey ahead of you. You will notice opportunities open up that continue to lead you in a specific direction. There will be many chances to say yes. My keyword for the Chariot is *focus*. You must stay focused on your intended goal, not allowing others' opinions or your own self-judgment to get in the way. Emotional outbursts are unacceptable. It is a time to take in, reflect, and process, but not to react. Stay focused. If you are not focused, neither are the horses or sphinxes leading the way, and then all is lost. All in all, this is a card of optimistic and successful opportunity, leading one toward a desired goal.

As I have stated before, I follow my tarot year energies with much focus and intention. During my most recent Chariot year, I started my potion-making business. This was the year in which I saw my products go into three stores and sell. I had the opportunity to teach and talk about my products, and they were truly born that year as a new being in the world. I took on the philosophy of "just say yes," and I used that word often during this year. I was offered the opportunity to teach some classes on essential oils and the elements, and I started reading tarot in a very difficult shop to get into as a reader. I said yes, I took every step I could forward, and I set a great foundation for myself and my business in the tarot and aromatherapy world. During this time I set out to find my place in the world, and I succeeded in laying new ground for future journeys.

Energies of the Chariot

- opportunity
- movement
- focus
- intention
- emotions
- protective shell
- victory

The Chariot's Essential Oil: Lemon Balm

ELEMENT: Water

ASTROLOGICAL INFLUENCE: Cancer

SCENT DESCRIPTION: Sweet citrusy lemon scent, very uplifting and joyful. Light, airy, smooth, and flowing with a sour note to the base.

I chose lemon balm (*Melissa officinalis*) essential oil for many reasons. Lemon balm is a water element oil with calming, soothing energy that helps mellow the nerves. Lemon balm is uplifting and calls in happiness of spirit. Using lemon balm during the Chariot energies can help one let go of emotional energies that are disrupting thought and process, so lemon balm can help one stay on track and not react to outside emotional and internal emotional disturbances.

Lemon balm is also part of the mint family, carrying the energy of clarity and focus. Using lemon balm allows one to stay focused on the road ahead. As Sandra Kynes states in her book *Mixing Essential Oils for Magic*, lemon balm calls in clarity and can help you find your purpose. Lemon balm carries the energies of growth and longevity, allowing you to carry out your desired goal.

Lemon balm is processed through steam distillation of the leaves and tiny flowers from the plant, so there is also the energy of attraction in this oil from the flowers. Lemon balm calls in and attracts fertility (growth) and success. With the sweetness of this oil, its ability to attract, and its calming and uplifting energies, as well as its ability to open up the mind for clarity and focus, I feel that lemon balm is the perfect match for the Chariot.

THE CHARIOT TEA
    1 teaspoon dried lemon balm leaf
    1 teaspoon dried hawthorn leaf
    1 teaspoon dried damiana leaf
    1 teaspoon dried spearmint leaf
    1 teaspoon dried holy basil
    ¼ teaspoon dried orange peel

Mix together, then add one teaspoon of the mix to a tea strainer. Cover with hot water and allow to sit for 3–5 minutes. Add honey if desired.

Downsides of the Chariot

- wrong direction
- weakness of will
- overly emotional
- lack of focus
- running wild

Support from the Council of Queens

I feel that there are two queens who may be able to help you through this energy of the Chariot.

The Queen of Pentacles grounds your energy. You are traveling on the road to your success, so staying sure-footed and strong are key ingredients to survival. The Queen of Pentacles can make you strong and serious about your journey, not allowing one to veer off-track.

The Queen of Swords is the least emotional queen. She does not mess around. She can bring in more clarity and focus as well as inspiration for your journey. She can be harsh with her words, she will not let you fail, and she can help keep your emotions in check.

The Queen of Wands can light the spark within you to keep you motivated and give you the confidence to continue on your journey with passion and the desire to get to where you are going.

The Queen of Cups is water element and already flowing through the Chariot's veins, but if you wish, call her in to support listening to your intuition.

Companion Card

The Chariot is number 7 in the tarot. The companion card would be the Tower, number 16: $1 + 6 = 7$. The Tower will be of service to the Chariot because it assists in lessons of failure and defeat. Although there may be failure, there is also knowledge and new ground formed by that failure. As the Chariot teaches, we must keep going and stay focused; we do not have time to wallow in defeat because we still have more roads to travel, and we will forge forward with victory in sight. The Tower is a reminder of what can happen when we are not focused or when we lose sight of the destination. When we focus on the ego instead of the whole, we are in Tower time. The Tower is a looming reminder of what can happen when our ego crashes because we are not driving with integrity. It also reminds us to let go of what needs to be released before it tumbles.

Strength

NUMBER: 8

ELEMENT: Fire

ASTROLOGICAL INFLUENCE: Leo

A Message from Strength

It is time to really trust yourself. You know what to do. You know what is right. This may be a difficult time in which you must also be open to trust in and receive guidance from something larger than yourself. With unconditional love for yourself and those around you, with compassion and an open heart, you will find your truth. Trust yourself. It is time to own all of your being and realize that sometimes the dark is as beautiful and important as the light. You are a beautiful and magical being: know that. All in all, you will find your strength.

Meanings

If you have chosen the Strength card or Strength has chosen you, it is time to own yourself. It is time to love yourself: all of you. Embrace the darkness within. Do not tame the beast within but befriend the beast within. You are beautiful, all of you. This is a time of possible uprooting in some way, and the key is to be rooted no matter what is going on around you. You may have to make some difficult choices, and the key here is to remember to trust your decision. Trust and embrace your choices. This is a time to be open to receive as well as give. You are strong, and you have courage. In the *Druid Craft Tarot*, the authors explain Strength as "wild wisdom," and this is where Strength comes from and feels like. There is a raw internal knowing, a wisdom from within that leads you to make wise and truthful choices. If you listen and trust yourself, you will find the peace, courage, and strength that resides within.

I don't believe I will ever forget my Strength year. To date it has been one of the most powerful and blessed years I have ever had.

When I reached my Strength year it was quickly apparent that I was going to need to be strong, grounded, and have faith in myself. That quality of self-trust was needed. Needless to say, the year started off with a bang. First, I ended up in the hospital, waiting to find out if I would need to have surgery to remove part of my colon due to an abscess and a tear. I was fortunate and it healed without surgery. Within the next month or so, after recovering from the illness, it became fairly obvious that my little white dog was ill. She was fourteen years old, and her belly had become rather large and she could not hold her bladder well. At times she was in pain. I had to come to terms that it was her time to pass on. It was the most dreaded and difficult decision that I had been under pressure to handle in some time. I spoke with my dog and read to her about dogs and the rainbow bridge. I slept downstairs on the couch with her so that I could clean up after her or rush her outside when needed. I stayed by her side as much as I could until it was apparent she was ready to go. Her passing was peaceful as we had her doctor come to our home and administer the medications. She went in peace, and I was at peace.

Just about two weeks before my little dog left, I was outside on the back deck with her. She let me know that she wanted to go out in the woods to do what dogs do and I realized that I did not have any shoes on. My husband gave me his big shoes to wear, and I started down the steps of the back porch with my little dog in tow. As I looked down at my feet, déjà vu came over me and I saw myself as a little girl walking around the house in my father's big shoes. At that moment I heard my father say, "I know you are sad that she is leaving you, but I want you to know that I will be there for her. I will lift her up, and she will know no fear." When I heard this, my heart was at peace. My father loved dogs, so who better to be there for her? My little dog's death was a great lesson in strength. The courage it takes to let go of a loved one is a strength I understand in losing my father, my mother, and my little white dog.

There was more to lose and gain in my Strength year. After my little dog had left us, my husband got a new job in the city. Now this would be about an hour and a half commute one way for him, and we thought we would just let him settle and then we would decide what to do from there. Well, not even three days after my husband was hired, I received a phone call from a specialist's office offering me a job in the city. I said it must be meant to be, so I took the job. We quickly found an apartment in Portland and started getting the house ready to sell. We lived up at the foothills of Mt. Hood in a small town in Oregon, and our home was a 1920s cabin on the river. Keeping it up without us living there would be difficult, so we put the house up for sale. It sold in one day for cash and for our asking price.

This left me with another predicament. We were moving into a one-bedroom apartment in the city and I had my cat, Kitten. Kitten was mainly an indoor cat, but she liked to venture out into the woods around our home. She would stay close, but I knew she would not do well in a one-bedroom apartment. I had to find her a new home. This broke my heart. I found her a great home and was able to receive pictures of her happy self on occasion.

What a busy and draining year! Within less than two months, everything I had known within the last seventeen years had changed. My home, my job, even my pets were either gone or in a different home now. It took courage and faith in myself to maneuver through this year. My message to myself was to stay rooted, no matter what is occurring around me.

Here is what I have to say about Strength in my personal experience of it. Strength is courage. Strength is this internal knowing that allows you to do what you need to do. Strength supports you—all of you. It cradles you. It allows you to look at the darker half of your being and have compassion and unconditional love for all of you. Strength supports your spirit, your body, and your mind. When you feel the power and the energy of Strength and allow it to encompass your being, you can then share the qualities of Strength with your loved ones and all that you are in community with.

This is what I felt in my Strength year when I had many difficult, heartrending decisions to make. I had to let go and let spirit and my father take the wheel. I had to be rooted in myself, no matter where life took me. I felt as if I was Dorothy in *The Wizard of Oz*, being uprooted and moved away from everything I had known for the last seventeen years, and yet there was this sense of peace and knowing within and around me. There was a knowing that this was the time and this was the season for all this shifting energy.

Energies of Strength

- strength
- courage
- rootedness
- passion
- compassion
- love
- power
- trust
- internal knowing
- love of self
- unconditional love

Strength's Essential Oil: Ginger

ELEMENT: Fire

PLANETARY INFLUENCE: Mars, Moon

SCENT DESCRIPTION: Ginger has a pungent, spicy, yet refreshing scent that is very strong and powerful with almost a powerful spicy hot bitterness to it.

I chose ginger because of its fire element energies and the fact that it is a root oil. When you eat ginger, it tends to warm the body, and in this way it gives comfort and physical energy. This is an outward-moving energy; like fire, it expands. Yet this oil comes from the root of the plant, which gives it a grounded, rooted, and earthy cradle to keep the flame. This gives the magical energy of being grounded yet expansive at the same time. Ginger is a cleanser and helps purify personal energy and the body as well as emotional energies. Ginger's healing quality lends support in general but also can help with working through and around obstacles and relationships. Ginger gives a sense of well-being. Although there may be fire all around and within, ginger sends in a knowing that all will be well. Ginger is strong and brings in courage, grounding, and vitality.

STRENGTH TEA

1 teaspoon black tea

¼ teaspoon ground ginger

A pinch ground cardamom

A pinch ground cinnamon

A pinch ground nutmeg

Put it all together in a strainer, pour hot water over it, and allow to sit for 3 minutes. Add a milk of your choice. This is one of my favorite morning teas for power and strength.

Downsides of Strength

- fear

- inability to accept all of one's self

- fear of one's self

- lack of trust

- immobility in a time of needed courage

Support from the Council of Queens

I would first call in the Queen of Pentacles for grounding, solidity, trust in self, and growth. With Strength energy things can feel out of control, so being centered is key with this card. The Queen of Pentacles will also give you space for your fire to burn safely and controlled. She will support the burn and help you build upon your strength.

My second choice would be the Queen of Swords for clarity and inspirational support. Call upon the angels and guides to help lead you through this energy, and ask the Queen of Swords to keep your mind stable and clear. She will also help to support Strength through words and communication as well as keeping one in line. Not too much air element, though, or the flames can be fanned too high for comfort. Ask this queen for clarity and support but not for expansion. There is enough expansion with the fire element.

The Queen of Cups can assist with emotional support during this time. She can help you to tune into your intuition and call in compassion for self and others. She can also call in a cooling effect for the fire element.

The Queen of Wands is already with you on this journey because Strength and this queen are both fire element. If you want to pull in a bit of extra energy from the Queen of Wands, call in courage to trust in yourself and your decisions as you move forward.

Companion Card

Strength is number 8 in the tarot. Sometimes Justice is number 8 and Strength is 11, depending upon the deck. The companion card would be the Star, number 17: $1 + 7 = 8$. The Star may be the card of advice for the Strength card. During the energy of the Strength card, we can find difficult and challenging energies that require strength, unconditional love, compassion, and courage to move through and walk through. The Star calls in the energy of hope, inspiration, and internal well-being, allowing for belief and trust in self to make and trust in the decisions that are needed during this time.

The Hermit

NUMBER: 9

ELEMENT: Earth

ASTROLOGICAL INFLUENCE: Virgo

A Message from the Hermit

I am the Hermit, and I walk the long path of life, experiencing and gathering knowledge along the way. Integrity, honesty, and stillness within are required tools for the journey. One day I will look back from where I have come and I will remember my lessons and earned wisdom. All the hidden treasures that were secured along the journey are now valuable gifts that have taught me the mysteries of life. At this point I will become the guide for others, leading the way with my lantern. I am the knowledge of life lived. I am the sage who leads with integrity, for those who lead without integrity will lead others astray. Remember to practice what you speak.

Meanings

If you have chosen the Hermit or the Hermit has chosen you, it is time to seek wisdom from within. The Hermit could be asking you to step into your cave of silence and wisdom and listen. There is much to be learned from within. This is a time of reflection, meditation, and peaceful quiet. This could also be a time for an internal journey, stepping into the underworld to communicate with your ancestors or guides for wisdom.

The Hermit could also be asking you to seek wisdom from a sage, an elder, or a spiritual teacher—from someone who is wise beyond your years. Someone to study with. Or are you the Hermit? Is it time for you to step into your wisdom and become the guide for others? Are you the teacher, the wise one, the guide? If you are being asked to step into the role of teacher or are being asked for advice from others, then you may need to take out your lantern.

The Hermit is the number 9 card of the major arcana, so we are almost at 10. What needs to be completed before we move to number 10 and the Wheel of Fortune's turns with new beginnings? Time to finish up so that the path can be cleared for departure.

The Hermit gives you the advice to finish things up before you move on. I remember in my Hermit year I did just that. By my Hermit year, I had designed five different oil blends, one for each queen in the tarot, and I had designed a moon blend. I had been working hard to come up with a firm foundation for my blends, and I was ready to take them on a new adventure but was not sure what that was at the time. I also took my aromatherapy boards during my Hermit year and passed my exam, becoming a full-fledged aromatherapist. I was ready for the real world! I spent some time searching my soul for what needed to be finished and where I wanted to go next in my life. This discovery had been difficult for me in the past, but now I was more secure in who I was. I trusted my intuition to lead the way. The Hermit has to walk the path first. The Hermit has to learn and take in as well as understand before he can become the guide for others to follow.

Energies of the Hermit

- wisdom
- knowledge
- understanding
- intuition
- the cave within
- completing unfinished tasks

- meditation
- stillness
- quiet
- integrity
- honesty

The Hermit's Essential Oil: Spanish Sage

ELEMENT: Earth, air

PLANETARY INFLUENCE: Jupiter, Mercury

SCENT DESCRIPTION: Spanish sage has an herbaceous scent yet is light and airy, with a slight lavender quality.

I chose Spanish sage for the Hermit because sage chose me. I was searching for the right oil for the Hermit, and every time sage would pop up, I would automatically say "the Hermit" after reading the energies. Sage is a sacred and ancient plant that has been used for spiritual purposes as well as opening up the third eye for divination and contacting ancestors and guides. According to *The Flower Essence Repertory* by Patricia Kaminski and Richard Katz, sage is good for gathering one's wisdom from life experiences and then looking at life from a higher perspective.

We all know of the sacred burning of sage to purify and protect by many American Indians. Working with sage not only connects us to the higher realms for inspiration and wisdom, but sage can purify our energies and put a shield of protection around us as well. Sage is believed to support longevity and aging. As one ages, sage helps to bring a peaceful and quiet acceptance to the aging process and allows for wisdom. Working with sage brings the ability to process and cleanse challenges that meet us along our life path, allowing us to investigate as well as purify the energy. This helps carry the learned wisdom with us.

I am currently working with Spanish sage, and it is lovely. Spanish sage is a middle note oil and is listed in the herbaceous scent group. Sage blends well with other herbaceous oils as well as woody and citrus oils.

Burning Sage

Purchase a sage bundle and use it to clear the energy of your home and your body. Not only does it smell lovely, it allows for a new open container for your creative spirit and knowledge to surface.

Downsides of the Hermit

- immaturity
- fear of aging
- loneliness
- isolation
- preaching without practicing

Support from the Council of Queens

If one is having difficulty with isolation and loneliness, I would call in the Queen of Swords for inspiration and connection through writing. This is a time of solitude, and being alone can be difficult for some. The Queen of Swords can give you inspiration for your alone space. Keeping a journal and communicating through the pen helps open up channels for support. This queen will also help keep one in line so that all that needs to be completed before moving on and changing is done to perfection.

The Queen of Cups can help open up emotions, allowing for release of bound-up space in the body. Allowing for a flow during this time helps to connect with spirit and one's guides. The Queen of Cups can allow for intuition to become full force so that all that needs to be answered and healed can come to the forefront, allowing for new freedom and opening space for new beginnings.

Call in the Queen of Wands to help with completion. The Hermit is number nine within the major arcana. The number nine is about completion. What needs to be finished up before moving into the energy of the ten? Call in the fire of the Queen of Wands to create energy, passion, and desire. She will help you create and finish what needs to be completed. She will also give you the courage to transition from the number nine and into the energy of the ten, change.

Although the Hermit is of the earth element, as is the Queen of Pentacles, possibly embracing the grounding effects of touching the earth and being here now is something this queen can help with. The Hermit often lives within his cave. He is in a place of internal dwelling. The Queen of Pentacles can get him out of the cave and into reality, therefore allowing him take those grounded steps toward completion and move forward on his path of knowledge in the real world.

Companion Card

The Hermit is number 9 in the tarot. The companion card would be the Moon, number 18: $1 + 8 = 9$. The Moon may be an advice card for the Hermit. The Moon can help call in and embrace its feminine energies. The Moon will help the Hermit connect to this feminine side and step deeper into his intuitive well of knowledge. The Moon can help you encounter and work with the shadow side of your being. Call in psychic ability. Call in the ability to walk in the dark, to see what cannot be seen except through the internal intuitive flow of the Moon.

The Wheel of Fortune

NUMBER: 10

ELEMENT: Fire

PLANETARY INFLUENCE: Jupiter

A Message from the Wheel of Fortune

I am the Wheel of Fortune. I offer you change. As the seasons change and the years go by, you will change with them. Time does not wait. What goes up must come down, and what is down will rise again. Where are you on the wheel? Are you rising or are you falling? You are at a turning point in your life, and outside forces are manifesting change. All in all, I am a positive energy, offering opportunity and progression forward. Will this change bring you closer to your destiny? This may be a time when all of your hard work is paying off. Accept the change and gain control of your destiny. Karma is at work here.

Meanings

If you have chosen the Wheel of Fortune or the Wheel of Fortune has chosen you, then you are at a turning point in your life. Change is coming. These are the times we are only in control of before they happen and after they have shown themselves. Sometimes we set up change and sometimes we have no control over the changes that occur in our life. The key here is to accept the change and gain your own control over how you work with the change.

I will never forget my most recent Wheel of Fortune year. I was turning fifty-five and was at my first Tarot Symposium on my birthday. I was there selling my potions, and it was so wonderful; I had never experienced anything like this. So many magical and like-minded souls in one spot; so much fun! I decided that for my birthday I was going to buy a new deck as a gift to myself. I had my eye on this amazing deck that only consisted of the major arcana. This deck was $100. It was so beautiful and it was my birthday, so I bought it. The deck came in a beautiful gold box and with a free tarot reading. When I purchased my gift, I noticed that my box was numbered 55: exactly my new age. The reading was awesome in that the Wheel of Fortune came up and the Magician came up. I remember thinking, I am turning 55 today and I received deck number 55. If you add together $5 + 5$, you get 10, hence the Wheel of Fortune. If you add together $1 + 0 = 1$, the Magician. So in that moment, I decided to work with the Magician as my guide for the year to help me manifest the changes that I wanted to see in my Wheel of Fortune year.

During this year I ended up changing jobs and working closer to home. I worked on getting my potions into more stores, and I decided that I wanted to write and I wanted to get my writing published. It worked. By the end of the year, I had my potions in several shops, and a quarterly tarot journal had published four of my articles and picked up another in the following year. Through this year I learned that change happens: it may be out of our control or it may be orchestrated by us. Either way, when change happens we must accept and create from that change. I learned that although I am not always in control of what happens, I am in control of how I work with that energy. I can be defeated or I can be completed.

Change is not always bad. Change can be magical and uplifting. With my Wheel of Fortune year, my changes were all positive; I just needed to be aware of the energies surrounding me and call in my own forces of change. Change happens: be aware of the energies of change and gain control. You are a powerful being and you have the ability to manifest the changes you wish to see in your life.

Energies of the Wheel of Fortune

- change
- turning point
- destiny
- harvest
- synchronizing
- ending
- beginning
- prosperity

The Wheel's Essential Oil: Black Pepper

ELEMENT: Fire

PLANETARY INFLUENCE: Mars

SCENT DESCRIPTION: Spicy and energizing, light with a slight citrus to it.

I chose black pepper for its fire element energies and the fact that the oil is created through steam distillation of the unripe peppercorns, which are round in shape like the Wheel of Fortune. Black pepper is a stimulant and helps open the mind as well as increase energy to the body. Black pepper brings in clarity and focus for the changes that are occurring in the time of the wheel. The spiciness of this oil will help keep one moving forward, not allowing for inertia. Black pepper calls in the energies of determination, outward movement, expansion, and courage, and it is quite helpful for protection and banishment of unwanted energies that are holding you back from your desired destiny. I love the scent of this oil in that it is spicy yet light and uplifting. There is almost a slight citrus to the scent. Black pepper is in the spicy scent group and blends well with other spicy oils as well as woody, resinous, or citrus scents.

The Cauldron Meditation

I love to journey to the underworld, and in one of my imaginative journeys, I found a magic cauldron within. In this journey, I was walking through the jungle with a tiger by my side. The tiger said, "Follow the snake." I then saw a beautiful creamy yellow boa constrictor that was heading toward its lair. I followed the boa and saw myself meditating in the boa's lair. Soon the boa swallowed me. Next I was a beautiful tree within the jungle. I had bright red leaves for my hair and the trunk of the tree was covered in the skin of the snake. Within the belly of the tree was a cauldron and it was boiling, bubbling, and steaming up to the heavens. At that point it was time to come out of the journey.

A couple of months later, I read about the Celts and their many uses for the cauldron. One of the uses is the Cauldron of Transformation. I decided to work with the cauldron as it was shown to me in the journey I described above. This cauldron was in my pelvic region and solar plexus, and it was steaming and boiling. This is your will to become. I now do a meditation with the cauldron and teach this meditation to clients that I am reading for. I envision this cauldron in my belly bubbling and steaming up to the heavens, and in this cauldron I place my dreams, my passions, my ambitions, and my desires. I send these requested prayers up to the heavens to become. I throw anything that I no longer need or is hampering my desires in the flames beneath the cauldron to be composted for those who are requesting these energies for themselves. In this manner nothing goes to waste. I used this cauldron during my Wheel of Fortune year to manifest the changes I wished to see within myself as well as in my environments. It worked.

Downsides of the Wheel of Fortune

- unwilling to accept change
- difficulty letting things go
- stress
- loss
- difficulties
- misfortune

Support from the Council of Queens

The Wheel of Fortune is full of fire, so working with one of the other queens to help you through the energy may be required. The Queen of Pentacles can add grounding during this time of change. She will counsel you on how to dig deep and root, as well as how to set up boundaries when needed and how to help create abundance during this time.

The Queen of Cups can help with intuition, divination, releasing grief, and allowing one's feelings to flow. She can also help with trust of self and knowledge of the mysteries.

The Queen of Swords can bring in clarity, vision, and truth. She will help you cut through the muck and make things clear, allowing for movement forward without fear, and she will help get things done quickly and precisely.

If you wish to just work with fire, then you are in good form already with the wheel. You can call in the Queen of Wands if you wish to add some magic to the fire. She will help you create those spells.

Companion Cards

The Wheel of Fortune is number 10 in the tarot. The companion cards would be the Sun (19) and the Magician (1)—think the Sun = 1 + 9 = 10 and the Magician number 1 as the Wheel reduces down to 1: 1 + 0 = 1. Calling upon the Magician or the Sun for support may be an option. Working with the Magician can help you manifest the changes you wish to see in your life. Write down all that you want to accomplish in this year. Ask the Magician to be your guide and create the world you wish to live in. The Sun will call in the energy of success and individuality. Allow yourself to be seen and to shine. Work with the Sun to show your true self, be free of limiting beliefs, and create success.

Justice

NUMBER: 11
ELEMENT: Air
ASTROLOGICAL INFLUENCE: Libra

A Message from Justice

I am Justice, and I bring clarity, balance, and linear movement. This is now a time to put things in order and bring life into balance. When my energy encompasses you, there may be legal issues to work through or a business to put in order. Make sure that everything you do during this time is done precisely in order to manifest your will. Make sure that any contract is fair to you as well as to others that may be involved. Are the scales that represent your life balanced or are they tipping in one direction that is causing discomfort in your life? I am air, and I can help make things clear; together we create balance. Justice is about finding balance in one's outer world.

Meanings

If you have chosen Justice or if Justice has chosen you, it is time to get any legal issues in order as well as take a look at your external life for imbalance. Often we are focusing too much in one direction and forgetting about the other aspects of our life. Maybe it is time for some meditation and clarity.

This is a time for perfectionism. Make sure that you dot all the i's and cross all the t's. At this time cut away anything that is not right for you or anything that is taking control over you and not allowing for exploration in the other areas of your life. Now is the time to face reality and make sure everything is in its place and has been valued and respected. With clarity and confidence, you can move forward on your journey knowing that all is in order. Finding balance in your life calls in the energies of stability, confidence, control, and power, as well as being open to receive energy from all four elements. Truth, clarity, and fairness are keywords to remember when working with Justice.

In my Justice year, I made my business legal. I got a business license and tax ID as well as insurance and an accountant. Making things right, keeping things in order, and allowing for advice from others was my focus. By allowing others to take on some of the responsibility for me, such as the accountant, I was allowing for some freedom in my life as well as setting a strong foundation for growth. Now I could open up energies in other areas that had previously taken up my focus. Balance brings security. I like to look at the elemental energies that surround me, those of earth, water, fire, and air. What aspects of my life fall into these elemental energies, and how am I managing in those fields of energy? Is my water element out of control? Is there emotional stress or imbalance? Do I need to look at my relationships? How can I bring those energies into balance? I like to do a full external body scan and see where my imbalances lie and how I can bring them into a cohesive fit. What energies are surrounding me right now, and how can I restore balance in these areas?

The Justice card is an air element card, so focusing on mental, practical, and legal issues during this time is key. Once these energies are in order, other elemental energies will begin to open up and find some balance.

Energies of Justice

- truth
- clarity
- balance
- legal matters

- critical mind

- perfectionism

- law

- judgment

- getting it done

- finance

Justice's Essential Oil: Rosemary

ELEMENT: Air, fire

ASTROLOGICAL INFLUENCE: Leo

SCENT DESCRIPTION: Rosemary is a light and airy
herbaceous scent with a slight minty, medicinal
energy.

I chose rosemary mainly because of its energy of clarity, focus, and memory retention. I feel that with the focused energy of this oil, rosemary will keep one in line and moving forward with one's desired intention. Rosemary cracks the whip and says, "Let's get this done correctly and in a timely manner." Rosemary is also very good for banishing, and this is helpful in removing unwanted energies as well as aspects of one's life that are no longer useful and are therefore unhelpful in creating balance. Rosemary is considered a fire oil because of its relationship to Aries, Leo, and the Sun, but rosemary is also related to the air element through its association with Aquarius and the fact that the oil is part of the mint family. Rosemary opens the mind and leaves space for clarity, communication, inspiration, focused thought, intention, and memory retention. Rosemary is in the herbaceous scent group and blends well with other herbaceous oils as well as woody and citrus oils.

JUSTICE TEA

> 1 tablespoon dried rosemary leaf
>
> 1 tablespoon dried spearmint leaf
>
> 1 tablespoon dried gotu kola leaf
>
> 2 tablespoons dried holy basil

Combine herbs together and mix. Use 1 heaping teaspoon per cup. Place herbs in a tea strainer and cover with hot water. Steep for 3–5 minutes, or until the tea is a golden color. This tea is great hot or iced.

Downsides of Justice

- injustice
- prejudice
- dishonesty
- lack of clarity
- imbalance

Support from the Council of Queens

Calling in the Queen of Swords for support may be necessary with this card. Although Justice is an air element energy, the Queen of Swords can help you face reality and get to work. She will not allow you to ignore or hide from what needs to be completed. She will help with communication, clarity, focus, and intention, as well as keep you in line and moving in the right direction.

The Queen of Pentacles will root you down and set you out to task, setting a firm foundation for you to walk upon.

Call in the Queen of Wands to create the energy and passion you may require to get things in order. At times we need to get things done but we just don't have the drive to do it. Use this queen's magic to help call in the right tax accountant, banker, or lawyer for your plans. Use her charisma to attract just what you need in your life to succeed in finding order.

Call in the Queen of Cups to support your intuition during this time of finding order and balance. Ask her for support of the heart in knowing what you need to let go of and what needs to stay in your life and be organized. She will help you open your heart and see what you cannot possibly let go of and what truly needs to be released.

Companion Cards

Justice is number 11 in the tarot. It sometimes is number 8, depending upon the deck (some decks associate Justice with 8 and Strength with 11). I stick with number 11 for Justice, so based on that numerology, the companion cards would be Judgment, number 20, and the High Priestess, number 2. Judgment's 20 reduces down to 2 $(2 + 0 = 2)$ and Justice's 11 will also reduce down to 2 $(1 + 1 = 2)$. Both the High Priestess and Judgment could be advice cards for Justice.

The High Priestess can help with trusting your intuition to help make balanced decisions during this time. She can help you see clearly what needs adjusting.

Judgment can show you that through creating balance in your life, you have the opportunity for new beginnings and clarity about where your path is leading. Judgment can sometimes be just that: at times you can feel the weight of Judgment upon you, and this can be a key element during your Justice year. Justice asks for balance and order. Judgment can help you determine what is right for you and help you transition and create the changes and adjustments that are required for movement forward.

The Hanged Man

NUMBER: 12

ELEMENT: Water

PLANETARY INFLUENCE: Neptune

A Message from the Hanged Man

I am the Hanged Man, and I surrender. I have chosen to let go and let spirit be my guide. I will no longer fight because I know that I need not do so. As I let go, I release all that is clouding my vision and body. In this manner I allow for an opening and expansion of spirit within and without my being. As I hang here on the Tree of Life, I gain spiritual wisdom; I can now look at the situation in a different manner. I may not see this world or situation as others would, but I trust the wisdom of spirit as it flows through me. I am in suspension, hanging in the betwixt and the between. There is sacred energy here with me. There are times in life when one cannot be in control. We are not always the driver of our destiny. We feel as if we are wading through waist-deep water and we are not getting to our destination. This time warp seems never-ending, but remember that we are being guided and sometimes the best solution is to let it be, let it go, and find a new perspective.

Meanings

If you have chosen the Hanged Man or the Hanged Man has chosen you, then you may be in a time of suspension or it may be time to just let go, move on, and look at things differently. Build upon what is now, not what might have been. I had a difficult time reading this card until I lived it and I watched others move through it.

During my daughter's Hanged Man year, she felt as if nothing at all happened. She was in a holding space. She could not move forward and she did not wish to go backward; she was in suspension.

It was not until her following year, her Death year, that she would experience the changes that were brewing in her Hanged Man year. I love how Benebell Wen speaks of the Hanged Man in her book *Holistic Tarot* as the unsettling calm before a storm—the storm being the card that follows the Hanged Man in the major arcana: the Death card.

For me it was totally different. My year started with me in a fog of confusion. I have hypothyroidism and had just finished going through menopause. Menopause had totally wacked my thyroid out of control, and my medications were off. I was a mess of depression and anxiety. I was deep down in the well and could not understand why. There were other energies in my life at the time that I was not open to welcoming. Someone had entered my life and I felt them sucking my energy dry. The problem was, this was not my friend but another family member's friend. I felt I was stuck with this person's energy, as it was not my place to ask this person to vacate my life. I felt as if I was drowning in tears. I felt like a victim. So I decided to not fight the energy with physical communication or negative energies. Instead, I worked on a spell to clear my home as well as bring the family closer together. This person was not family, so this person was excluded. As soon as I took to cultivating a better mental attitude, I called in my guides and ancestors to guide me through. I sent my invocation and spell out to the universe, and everything changed. The very next day, this person was gone from my life. It all worked out in the long run. The key for me was not to wallow and try to fight this person with negative energy but to let it be and call positive energies into my home and life.

The Hanged Man represents a time of initiation, of letting go and surrendering to what is. It may be a waiting period or a time to dig deep into the well of your emotions. Know this: when the Hanged Man enters your life, you are being asked to be patient and open your heart to peace. Possibly look at things with new eyes and surrender to what is, but also know that you will move through this with your own personal and spiritual power.

Energies of the Hanged Man

- surrender
- sacrifice
- perspective
- peace
- suspension
- deep emotional experience
- spiritual deepening

The Hanged Man's Essential Oil: Chamomile

ELEMENT: Water

PLANETARY INFLUENCE: Sun

SCENT DESCRIPTION: Roman chamomile has a lighter and airier scent than that of German chamomile. Roman chamomile is soft and light and is calming yet uplifting in character. German chamomile, also known as blue chamomile, is much deeper and stronger in scent. This lends the ability for German chamomile to be a base note as well as a middle note. The oil has a lovely blue color. I love blue chamomile in salves and Roman chamomile for adding to oil blends and just to inhale, as it is lovely.

I chose chamomile for its water element energies, as the Hanged Man is also water element, as well as for chamomile's calming, peaceful, and comforting qualities. As I mentioned above, my Hanged Man year was a bit overwhelming and deeply emotional.

Chamomile is so soothing and calming. It assists with sleep and upset. Chamomile helps one with emotional healing and can assist with clarity and peace of mind. Since chamomile is a water element energy, this oil can assist with intuition and connection to spirit.

CHAMOMILE TEA

Chamomile tea is a very soothing and relaxing tea. Drink this tea to help with nervous tension and call in peace of mind.

Downsides of the Hanged Man

- martyrdom
- victim
- unable to let go
- selfish
- lack of faith in self and/or spirit
- stubbornness

Support from the Council of Queens

Sometimes with the energy of the Hanged Man, one feels as if they are treading water and not moving anywhere. Calling in the Queen of Pentacles can create a strong foundation to stand and root oneself. Think of the lotus flower that rises up through the mud and water to create beauty of spirit. Although movement forward is not happening, there is the combination of earth and water for growth. I think of the water element here as the spiritual realm and earth as matter. Planting a seed of potential within the earth and allowing water to nourish and quench the thirst of that seed allows for an opening up of the spirit. Grounding and rooting like the lotus allows you to rise up through the water and breathe. This is like a spell. Here you are allowing for the energies of water (spirit) to affect earth (matter).

Calling in the Queen of Swords (air) allows for thought and clarity, inspiration and communication, as well as the determination to work through this journey. The Queen of Swords does not mess around. She will guide one through with clear thought processes to let go and let be as well as open up ideas for a new perspective and possible new direction.

The Queen of Cups is water element, just like the Hanged Man. The Hanged Man is asking you to surrender and let go, but sometimes the energy of this card can feel as though you are stuck and not moving forward. Call in the Queen of Cups to create a flow of movement through the stagnant waters of the Hanged Man. Ask for a stream of energy to break up any blockages that are not allowing you to move forward. You can also work with this queen to call in intuition and spiritual support by tapping into your psychic abilities to gain advice and support from your guides and angels.

When in the Hanged Man energy, we may feel a lack of passion and joy. We may need the fire elemental energy of the Queen of Wands to call in the sun. If you are in stuck mode, and the Hanged Man and his Neptune energy has clouded your thoughts and set up disillusion in your life, the Queen of Wands can call back the fire that will bring about expansion and courage. She can light the spark that can help you to move through the deep, dark waters. Think of lighting a candle in the dark. This is your power and courage coming back to life.

Companion Cards

The Hanged Man is number 12 in the tarot. The companion cards would be number 21, the World, and number 3, the Empress. All three cards when reduced would add up to 3. Calling upon the Empress and the World for support might be an option. Hanged Man energy can feel heavy, stagnant, and sometimes unmovable. The

Empress, being the Mother, can nurture and take care of you during this time. Although there may be stagnant energy, there is growth happening within, and the Empress will feed this growth. I like to think of a whole ecosystem within the body growing and developing new internal energy.

The World card helps open and expand the energy of the Hanged Man. This can help with changing perspective and seeing all the other options that are out there for you. The World card will show us our limitations and yet also show us the possibility of future success. Imagine that you are supported by the whole world. I often feel that the Hanged Man needs to be nurtured and guided into change. Both the Empress and the World can be the foundation for support, release, and internal growth.

Death

NUMBER: 13

ELEMENT: Water

ASTROLOGICAL INFLUENCE: Scorpio

A Message from Death

My name is Death, and I walk with all beings who live upon the earth. I am a part of life's journey. I enter your life to release and transform what is no longer needed, and in the process I transform you. The energy within this card is not generally about the death of a life form but often about the death of an aspect of your being. Think of the butterfly and the cocoon. We enter into the cocoon to be transformed, and we emerge anew, beautiful and full of life, as the butterfly.

Meanings

If you have chosen the Death card or the Death card has chosen you, there is transformation afoot. As Alejandro Jodorowsky states in his book *The Way of Tarot: The Spiritual Teacher in the Cards*, the Hanged Man can lead one through an internal emptying that purifies and then releases one's past. He also states that the Death card in the tarot is number 13, not 22. If the Death card was really an ending, it would have been numbered 22 and would be the final card of the major arcana instead of the World. I believe that this card is just that: a purification of the past and/or present in order to create space for transformation.

In all my sixty years, I have only had one Death year, and that was at fifty-eight years old. I have to admit I was a bit worried about the outcome and the journey through the Death card, but as I moved through the Death year, I noticed that there was nothing that felt out of place or traumatic at all. What I felt by the end of my Death year was peace. I had shifted. No longer was I striving to become; I just was, and I was totally okay with that. I found that I no longer wanted to be more than what I already was. I was happy in my life. I was willing to accept my journey as it was and as it will be. As Death had allowed me to let go of all that had passed and was no longer needed, I was free to just be me.

I have seen some Death years that are a bit more traumatic than mine. My daughter, for example, got accepted into grad school, only to find out a couple of months later that the program had been canceled due to the death of the professor who ran the program. Her father got very ill and was on the verge of death but pulled through, and her boyfriend of four years decided to leave and move out without notice. They only had three weeks left on their lease and she had to either take over the lease or move. She was shocked and totally at a loss. She ended up moving, meeting someone else to whom she is now engaged to, and starting her own business. Through this experience, she found that she no longer wanted to go to grad school; she wanted to focus on her online business, and she was so happy that her ex-boyfriend had left. He was not the right one. She had to let go and live. Death took away those things that she did not need in her life, and she was then free to find her way. Everything was much better in the long run.

So, in conclusion, the Death card is about release of the past or present circumstances to create space for transformation. It is a purification and clearing out of energies and experiences that are ready for death so that life can begin anew.

Energies of Death

- release

- transformation

- mutation

- cleansing

- purification

Death's Essential Oil: Cypress

ELEMENT: Earth, water

PLANETARY INFLUENCE: Pluto, Saturn

SCENT DESCRIPTION: Cypress is woody yet
uplifting and breezy. There is a slight peppery scent
and a sense of freedom.

I chose cypress essential oil for several reasons. Cypress trees like to grow in or near water. Some cypress trees grow near the ocean and some in swamps or lakes. Cypress trees like to have access to swampy or wet soil as well as full sunlight. The roots of the cypress tree are tolerant of wet soils. As we can see, cypress essential oil is related to both the water and earth elements through its attraction to water as well as its woody scent. Death is a water element energy. Cypress has been associated with death, purification, and grieving since ancient times. In Egypt cypress was linked to the god Osiris, who was believed to be the god of the dead. In Greece cypress was used in companionship with journeys to the underworld. It was said that if you found a group of cypress trees, you had also found the barrier between the earth and the underworld. Cypress also brings peace and solace during times of loss. Scrying with mirrors whose frames are made of cypress wood is said to be helpful for one wanting to see past lives. Cypress is also associated with the energies of change and transformation.

I absolutely love the scent of cypress essential oil, and I absolutely love the magical look of cypress trees as they twist and bend in the wind. Cypress essential oil is light, airy, breezy, and fresh. It blends well with other woody scents as well as with herbaceous, spicy, or floral scents. Cypress is a middle to base note.

Downsides of Death

- fear of change

- stagnation

- depression

Support from the Council of Queens

The Queen of Swords might be of assistance in helping find inspiration and truth during this time of release. She can bring a logical clarity to the situation as well as allow you to be truthful with yourself. She can also invite communication, such as writing and speaking.

The Queen of Pentacles can help one to find structure and grounding during this time of change. Stability in matter can help calm emotions when one is well rooted.

The Queen of Wands can help you light a fire to burn up what needs to be released and use magic to quickly complete the process of transformation.

Allow the Queen of Cups to be of assistance to you; listen to her advice. Trust your intuition and see that you can walk through the dark by allowing your internal voice to be your guide. This will give you a knowing that often change is accompanied by grace and what is still available to you once all has been released will be a clearing for new possibilities. The Queen of Cups can help you be open to receive as well as truly feel your emotions; by allowing them to flow, you therefore truly release and surrender to what is dying in your life.

Companion Cards

Death is number 13 in the tarot, so reducing 13, 1 + 3 = 4, would call in the energy of the Emperor. This calls in the energy of fire for purification and release. The Emperor is the father figure in the tarot, so here we call in support for transformation and change. The

Emperor will bring in a grounding energy for the release. Although the Emperor is fire element, he is also the number 4, which is a stabilizing force, a container for change. He is a leader who embraces life's changes.

We also find the energy of the Fool here. The Fool is number 22 (as well as being numbered 0) and also reduces to the number 4: $2 + 2 = 4$. The Fool will allow you to jump and release what needs to go. The Fool will allow for the feeling of new beginnings and an excitement for new adventure.

Temperance

NUMBER: 14

ELEMENT: Fire

ASTROLOGICAL INFLUENCE: Sagittarius

A Message from Temperance

I am Temperance, and I carry with me the energies of harmony, internal healing, peace, fluidity, and alchemy. I cool what is too hot, and I heat what has been too cool. I am a blending of the forces. As Justice was a balancing of the external, I am a balancing of the internal. I bring a tempering of the conscious with the unconscious. I create a flow within your life—a flow between the worlds above and below. I help balance whatever is seeking wholeness within. I am the in-between, the middle way. I blend the fire of the sun with the coolness of the ocean, and in this blending I bring a balancing of the self.

Meanings

If you have chosen Temperance or Temperance has chosen you, this is a time of creating internal harmony and blending the forces within and without. This blending creates a new wholeness. Temperance creates the ability to be in contact with your intuition and spiritual self while still being rooted and grounded to the earth. This may consist of pulling out the treasures you have hidden and gathered within yourself along the way that are now needed to create a new, balanced energy within, like clearing out the cupboards to create a new you. This is a reconciliation of the opposites within. This is a very creative time and a possible time for success. Pay attention to synchronicity, for there may be a message that leads to a new destination. After the powerful energy of the Death year, Temperance calls in a year of internal healing.

Energies of Temperance

- blending
- fluidity
- harmony
- peace
- balance
- alchemy
- magic
- middle way
- synchronicity

Temperance's Essential Oil: Juniper

ELEMENT: Fire, water

PLANETARY INFLUENCE: Mars, Sun, Mercury

SCENT DESCRIPTION: A woody and refreshing
scent with a bit of peppery spice.

I chose juniper for several reasons. Juniper is distilled from the
fruits of the juniper plant. This makes juniper a plant with the energy
of fire, and the fruit of the plant carries the energy of fruition, completion, and success. This oil is great for removing energies that need
to go and helping bring about healing and a sense of well-being. Juniper oil is great for protection, grounding, and spirituality, and it helps
with transformation. Juniper has been used for purification. This
gives us the knowledge that juniper is a powerful oil for clearing the
energies within so that a new blending can begin in preparation for
new beginnings. Think of juniper as the fire that burns a path within
so that the cool waters of healing can flow through and heal. Here we
are melding and tempering fire and water. Juniper has a lovely scent
that is sweet and fresh as well as woody. Juniper is in the wood scent

group and blends well with other woody scents as well as spicy, herbaceous, and floral scents.

Downsides of Temperance

- imbalance
- disharmony
- fragmentation
- falling apart

Support from the Council of Queens

With the Temperance card, we are working with the fire element. If we are truly working toward balance, then calling in the Queen of Cups to help support the blending would be good. She will open up one's intuition and psychic abilities, allowing for the flowing of fire and water together, side by side. Water will help enforce the healing and spirituality of the journey as well as open up communication with guides, personal intuition, and fluidity.

The Queen of Pentacles could be of service to help find the middle road and put one's feet upon the ground, centering the body and soul. She will help you be rooted while this spiritual blending is taking place within.

The Queen of Swords can help you find inspiration during this time, as well as focus and clarity, allowing you to be more aware of the synchronicities that may be surrounding you.

Temperance is a time of blending, alchemy, balance, and synchronicities. Call in the Queen of Wands to harness these magical energies and create whatever it is that you want in your life. Grasp onto those synchronicities and throw them in your cauldron. Now is the time to blend and create your brew. You are internally coming into balance. Bottle this energy for future use.

Companion Cards

Temperance is number 14 in the tarot, so reducing 14, $1 + 4 = 5$, calls in the energy of the Hierophant: tradition, higher education, spirituality, and conformity. Temperance is asking for internal healing, melding and tempering to blend into a new internal you. The Hierophant can help meld the spiritual energies with the physical body by calling in the spiritual for support, as well as to helping conform to the new middle way. While Temperance is a fire element energy that helps temper the internal, the Hierophant's earth element can be the foundation for change, with the external connection with spirituality and higher learning forming a grounded support system that allows for your personal development. Remember that the Hierophant can help you conform to the new melding within your being.

The Devil

NUMBER: 15

ELEMENT: Earth

ASTROLOGICAL INFLUENCE: Capricorn

A Message from the Devil

I am the Devil, and I am here to tempt you. I ask you to look deep within your darkness and ask: What am I attached to that is counter to my life and goals? What am I bound to that is not healthy to my body and soul? My message is "Don't be attached to the outcome," for attachment brings addiction. It is time to be devilish and have some fun, but be responsible, for you and only you can set yourself free.

Meanings

If you have chosen the Devil or the Devil has chosen you, it is time to enjoy the material aspects of your life. Be devilish and have some fun. Take a look at all the gifts you have been given in life and be grateful. Enjoy the earth, but be aware; with the Devil, we can take a look at the seven deadly sins: pride, greed, wrath, envy, lust, gluttony, and sloth. The question here is what or who has control over you? This is not a time to be attached to the outcome but to be free and limitless. It is time to break the bonds that hold you and set yourself free. This is a time of responsibility for self. Freedom brings peace of mind and the ability to truly be who you choose to see in the mirror. What are you bound to and how can you bring about freedom?

I remember doing a reading for my daughter right after she had graduated from college. She had her first real job as well as a new apartment. The card that really spoke during the reading was the

Devil. The message was that it was time to be responsible for herself as well as have some fun now and be a little devilish.

Energies of the Devil

- responsibility
- materialism
- temptation
- fun
- liberation
- self-discipline
- hard work

The Devil's Essential Oil: Angelica Root

ELEMENT: Earth

PLANETARY INFLUENCE: Sun

SCENT DESCRIPTION: Deep, earthy scent, almost like dirt itself and very herbaceous.

I chose angelica root because of its earth element energy and because angelica root is a powerful protector. Angelica root helps protect against evil and negative energies as well as call your angelic team to the rescue. Angelica is helpful in working through problems and calling in spiritual help. The root oil is helpful with grounding oneself and is associated with purification, stimulation, and success. Working with angelica root oil can be supportive in letting go of the bonds that tie, with support from the angelic realm as well as one's underworld allies. With the support of one's team, there can be a cutting of the cords, therefore allowing freedom to reign. Angelica root has a very deep, earthy scent, with almost a woody sweetness to it. Angelica is in the herbaceous scent group and blends well with other herbaceous oils as well as woody and citrus oils.

There is an angelica seed oil that also sits in the fire element and can be used to burn up any unwanted energies. This would work well with problems such as addictions and burning up the ties that bind.

Downsides of the Devil

- bondage
- addiction
- materialism
- jealousy
- selfishness
- obsession

Support from the Council of Queens

I really think you could call in any queen for help with this one. The Queen of Pentacles will help ground and center the mind and body, planting the seeds of success for dealing with any addictions or bonds that need breaking. She can also help with planting the seed for change as well as supporting self-nurturing.

Dealing with change and releasing what we have become accustomed to can be difficult. The Queen of Cups can help deal with the emotional side of the issues. She can create a gentle flow within your life to start a change or gently heal. Water is purification, allowing for healing and cleansing. The water element can also help one hone in on and trust one's intuition and psychic abilities. Call upon the Queen of Cups for healing and peaceful flow.

I like working with the Queen of Wands to create magic and to burn up unwanted stuff. Working with candle magic to create and banish is a powerful way to work with addiction or the release of something that is holding you up. This powerful queen can assist with creating the desired outcome through her magical gifts.

The wonderful Queen of Swords will set you straight. She will not mess with her words. For clarity and mental empowerment, call in the Queen of Swords.

Companion Cards

The Devil is number 15 in the tarot, so reducing the number 15, $1 + 5 = 6$, calls in the energy of the Lovers, which can help with shifting relationship energy as well as clarity of decisions. The Devil will help you see what you are bound to that is not healthy for you. The Lovers will help you determine if it is a relationship that is holding you back. The Lovers' energy will also help with choosing a clear direction in which to move. Remember that the Lovers card can represent being at a crossroads where there is a decision to be made. Cutting the bonds that hold and stepping onto a new, healthy path can be accomplished here.

The Tower

NUMBER: 16

ELEMENT: Fire

PLANETARY INFLUENCE: Mars

A Message from the Tower

*I am the Tower. I am here to shake you up and wake you up.
I will give you a good look at yourself. The lightning in the
card represents a jolt of power that destroys what is unreal
or ready to fall. I bring on sudden change that is hot and
fiery, and with this change I bring clarity. When lightning
strikes, it fertilizes the ground around it for new growth.
I am that lightning, and I welcome the new seeds to be
sown in order to create new ground. Sometimes I come
more quietly and there is a sudden clarity that brings
about a change, and sometimes I am chaos. I am here to
help you see what needs to be set free, let go of, or removed
so that one can begin to see clearly and plant the seeds of
new life. I may be unexpected and possibly unwelcome, yet
I come bearing the gift of clarity and a new day.*

Meanings

If you have chosen the Tower or the Tower has chosen you, all
I can say is don't fight it. The Tower brings about unexpected and
sometimes chaotic change. You may feel as if you have been left at
the altar, but if you were left at the altar, there was a reason for it.
The Tower can be a powerful and painful card, often staring you in
the face, clearly confronting you with your ego and your failures. At
other times the Tower is just an unexpected change that sends you
reeling in a new direction. Whatever the outcome, you are being
given the gift of looking at where you have been and what went
wrong or what needs to change in order to create anew. You now
clearly see the path before you.

I often think of a reading I did for a gentleman who came into my reading space and did not say a word. He did not have a question for the reading; he just knew that there was great change afoot. The first card I pulled for this man was the Tower. This card was placed in the spread representing him and where he was right then in his life. I finished the entire reading with no response from the man. As he got up to walk through the door to leave, he looked at me and said, "You know that first card you pulled, the Tower?" I said yes.

He said, "My girlfriend of seven years is moving out tomorrow, and I am in shock. I understand now that this is in the best interests of both of us. I am sorry and sad for the loss. I need to take a better look at myself." This is the energy of the Tower.

Energies of the Tower

- fire
- chaos
- change
- ego
- fertility
- power
- awareness

The Tower's Essential Oil: Coriander Seed

ELEMENT: Fire

PLANETARY INFLUENCE: Mars

SCENT DESCRIPTION: Coriander has an almost buttery scent to me that is soft and soothing, with a very slight sweetness and spiciness about it. It's a very lovely scent.

I chose coriander first because of its fire element energy and its affinity with the planet Mars and second because it is a very strong protector as well as a powerful tool for purification and release due to its fiery nature. Coriander helps you connect with your personal intuition and psychic powers as well as calls in courage and security. Coriander also is associated with change, allowing you to accept the movement that is happening around you and step forward in a new chosen direction with more power. Since coriander is a seed oil, you can use this oil to plant a new seed that enables you to walk through the fire of the Tower knowing that you will rise again with a new-found knowledge of yourself and where you are going.

Coriander is one of my favorite oils to diffuse in my home. Calling upon coriander to comfort yourself and release energies as well as to protect and instill courage can be an extremely powerful tool to have in your tool kit, especially during a time of chaos.

Downsides of the Tower

- chaos
- destruction
- fall of the ego
- loss
- reality

Support from the Council of Queens

During this time of chaos, some grounding would be great. Although one is standing on shaky ground during this time, calling in the Queen of Pentacles can bring in support. The Queen of Pentacles will take the new, fertile ground and nourish the seeds you plant for growth. She will also embrace you during this time as a child of her own. She will instill trust in self and allow for a rootedness within.

Calling in the Queen of Cups will help allow an emotional flow in life that will help release blockages. Releasing emotions and trusting in one's own gut during this time is very beneficial. This queen will help you walk through the dark forest of destruction with inner calm and knowing. The Queen of Cups will help you find your way through the dark. She will allow for spiritual connection and expansion of the heart chakra for embracing self.

Call in the Queen of Swords to bring clarity to the situation at hand. She can help you make logical decisions and not get entrenched in your emotions. This can be a difficult time in which your feelings and ego may be wounded. The Queen of Swords will not let you dwell on emotional energy. She will push you through the situation with a clearly focused mind.

Call in the Queen of Wands if you just really want to move through the fire of the Tower and burn everything up. She will help you destroy and move through the situation more quickly. Scorch and see what settles, then deal with the cleanup.

Companion Cards

The Tower is number 16 in the tarot, so reducing number 16 $(1 + 6 = 7)$ calls in the energy of the Chariot. The Chariot is water element, so you are adding in some cooling here for your emotions, allowing for you to move through the fire of the Tower and charge through without getting burned. Allow the Chariot to set a new course, a new direction, that allows you to release what is falling and leads to a new and clear foundation for future growth.

The Star

NUMBER: 17

ELEMENT: Air

ASTROLOGICAL INFLUENCE: Aquarius

A Message from the Star

I am the Star, and I am hope. I bring about an inner peace, a quiet. I am that sense of well-being that is now stirring within. As you accept and flow through the radiance of the Star, you start to glow, therefore sending out your own personal light. Through this light others will see that you are the Star, and they will follow. Just like the Star, you shine bright for others to see.

Meanings

If you have chosen the Star or the Star has chosen you, "hope" is the word that comes to mind. This Star shines from within you, and through you it exposes itself. There is an inner sense of peace, a knowing that all is well. Through this light within, you show the world a grace and beauty that all wish to obtain. It is time to shine, to be thankful for the world around you as well as within you. You are bright now for all to see. By allowing this light to flow from within you, the world will see and others will follow. Often the Star follows the Tower, which represents a time of peace and calm after the storm. There is a strength in this card for what you have endured, and now you have passed through the storm. All is well; you can internally feel the hope within. You have weathered the storm, and now you find peace.

Energies of the Star

- hope
- well-being

- peace

- calm

- inspiration

- spiritual abundance

The Star's Essential Oil: Violet Absolute
ELEMENT: Air, water
PLANETARY INFLUENCE: Venus
SCENT DESCRIPTION: A unique scent that is very
green and grassy with a very slight floral scent.

I chose violet absolute because it is an extremely lovely oil. It is one of my favorites in that it has such a deep, interesting scent. I call this one my spirit oil. To me, a spirit oil is individual for each person, based on individual preference. Violet absolute carries the energies of peace, hope, well-being, transformation, happiness, magic, and dreamwork, as well as spiritual abundance. This oil is magical. Violet has a deep, earthy scent almost like grass or moss, yet it has a slight floral energy. Violet carries the energy of the air element and is associated with Aquarius, as do the energies of the Star. Violet also has the energy of Venus and is sweet and loving to its wearer.

Violet absolute is extremely expensive, so I only purchase a very small amount at a time and always dilute. You don't need much for blending. Violet is also hard to categorize in a scent group; in researching this, the only time I found violet listed in a scent group, it was listed as a green scent or in the floral group, as I found in *Essence and Alchemy: A Natural History of Perfume* by Mandy Aftel. In our case we are going to think of it as a green/floral scent. Violet absolute is used mainly in perfumery as a fixative. It is generally not used in aromatherapy, but since we are creating magic potions, we can use it how we would like. Violet absolute will blend well with other floral scents as well as spicy, woody, and citrus scents. Again, only a small amount is necessary to incorporate the essence into a blend.

Downsides of the Star

- fear

- illness or health issue

- weakness

- lack of desire

- arrogance

Support from the Council of Queens

Since the Star is such a hopeful card, there is generally not much help needed here. The Queen of Cups can be of assistance to release any stored emotions that may need to go as well as allow for a flow of energy throughout the body to open the heart and heal. This queen will also help you follow your own intuition for self-trust and follow your dreams.

The Star energy is that of air. This means sometimes being up in the clouds for too long. Work with the Queen of Pentacles to ground your hope and sense of well-being. Bring it down to earth and share these energies with friends and family. With the Star as your archetype, you are shining bright; this may be of service to those who surround you. Reach out and make hope a reality for others.

Create magic by calling in the Queen of Wands. Hope is something we all need in our lives; I say bottle it up. We all need the energy of the Star at times. Use the charisma of the Queen of Wands to harness and share the Star's energy with others. Create a potion of hope or light a candle for hope and send hope out to the world.

The Queen of Swords can help you communicate hope. She will be an inspiration and help you write, sing, or speak about the beauty of hope. As the Star you will be received well and your message can be shared easily. Others will want to hear your message, so communicate through the Queen of Swords.

Companion Cards

The Star is number 17 in the tarot, so reducing number 17, $1 + 7 = 8$, calls in the energy of Strength, which is about owning all of oneself, the dark and the light, creating balance for well-being. In this time of hope and well-being, now is the time to call in the energy of Strength and own all of you, the external with the internal and the shadow with the light. Stand strong in who you are. Strength will also help you share the light of the Star with others through compassion and a grounded strength in self.

The Moon

NUMBER: 18

ELEMENT: Water

ASTROLOGICAL INFLUENCE: Pisces

A Message from the Moon

I am the Moon. As you walk through this journey, you will see that your path is not lit by the brightness of the Sun but by the glowing of the Moon, therefore you are walking through a reflection. You must now step forward trusting your intuition, your internal knowing, rather than your physical vision. You are stepping into the mystery, the unknown, the darkness, with only your intuition to lead the way. The hound and the wolf found on the traditional Rider-Waite-Smith card represent your fear, your beastly qualities, but as you step through these magnificent beasts, they become your allies. Now is the time to step through your fear and enter the darkness of the night, of the soul, and trust in yourself. You will find secrets and truth, fear and courage, danger and self-protection. You will seek within to find the answers. I will speak with you through dreams, images, memories, and emotional sensitivities, seeking to make the unconscious conscious.

Meanings

If you have chosen the Moon or the Moon has chosen you, it is a time of internal exploration. Step through your fears and step within yourself. This may be a time of emotional confusion, illusion, and deception, yet on this journey you will discover truth. Allow your imagination to speak, to flourish, to be open to new direction and change. This is not a time for escapism but for self-discovery. The Moon is number 18 in the tarot. If you reduce the number 18 to the number 9, you will find the Hermit, the companion to the Moon.

Ask the Hermit to be your guide through the darkness, and he will help light the way with his knowledge, wisdom, and lantern. He brings hope and illumination with the light of the Star (many decks show a star within the Hermit's lantern).

As the Hermit and the Moon are my birth cards, I personally understand the darkness and illusion of the nighttime. In not seeing the path clearly, one may struggle with their true destination. The path is not lit. This is a path of self-discovery. As you learn to trust the voice within, your fears will subside.

During this dark night of the Moon, you will need to call upon your own internal wisdom and intuition to find the path to the Sun.

Energies of the Moon

- darkness
- illusion
- imagination
- deep awakening
- stepping through fear
- isolation
- intuition
- seeing in the dark

The Moon's Essential Oil: Rose Geranium

ELEMENT: Water

PLANETARY INFLUENCES: Mars, Venus

SCENT DESCRIPTION: Very powerful scent that is floral, somewhat sweet, and very green and fresh.

I chose rose geranium essential oil because of its elemental energy of water as well as its powerful yet loving protective quality. I plant one rose geranium plant in each corner of my yard to help protect the property and home. Rose geranium is a mood stabilizer, giving it the ability to balance and calm emotions as well as help banish nightmares. It is calming as well as uplifting and carries the energies of courage and strength, allowing one to feel empowered, protected, and strong.

Rose geranium is very feminine in nature and calls in a flow that allows for movement of emotional energy within the body. I used a blend of rose geranium, lemon, myrtle, and patchouli as my menopause blend. After working with it for a while, I discovered that I felt calm and without emotional tension. I felt as if I could trust my intuition. This brought me strength and courage to move ahead. Rose geranium is in the floral scent group and blends well with other florals as well as woody, citrus, and resinous oils. Rose geranium has a very strong scent, so very little is needed in a blend as it will take over the other scents. Rose geranium will help to protect you on your journey as well as create courage, strength, flow, and beauty, and its feminine energy will call in personal wisdom and intuition.

Downsides of the Moon

- escapism
- delusion
- illusion
- fear
- depression
- lunacy

Support from the Council of Queens

The Queen of Pentacles will bring in grounding energy and a stability that may be required during this time of mystery and darkness. Being sure-footed in the dark is a good thing. Here is where you can embody the energy of this queen and call in the Hermit as a guide through the darkness, both being earth energy.

The Queen of Cups will help strengthen your intuition and psychic abilities. She will bring a flow throughout your journey and allow for healing. Although she is also the water element, she is the queen and has mastered her emotions, allowing one to feel and experience yet be calm and nonreactive to the unknown mysteries that lie ahead.

The Queen of Swords can help to bring clarity of mind, opening up the imagination and allowing for meditation.

The Queen of Wands can call in the courage to face the beasts that you may encounter. She can teach you to use the power of the wand to burn and transform them into compatible energies. Use the magical gifts and charisma of this queen to literally charm your fears into strengths.

Companion Card

The Moon is number 18 in the tarot, so it reduces via $1 + 8 = 9$ to the Hermit. Call in the energy of the Wise One, the Sage, to support your journey through the energy of the Moon. The Moon calls in a darkness, the unknown, and asks that you trust your intuition to move forward. The Hermit is your internal wisdom that will never let you down if you listen. Listen to the internal voice within to lead the way.

The Sun

NUMBER: 19

ELEMENT: Fire

PLANETARY INFLUENCE: Sun

A Message from the Sun

I am the Sun, and I bring fire, light, and joy. When you bask in my energies, you will find this joy and happiness shining within. There is freedom because you have nothing left to hide. You are free to be you. Open up your heart and lift your head toward the Sun. Feel the warmth upon your body and face. I have gifted you joy. Celebrate your life, celebrate your loves, your family, as well as your creative spirit. It is time to be grateful and joyous. Enjoy the Sun and enjoy your success.

Meanings

If you have chosen the Sun or the Sun has chosen you, it is time to be free, to rejoice. In the traditional Rider-Waite-Smith deck, the Sun card is depicted by a naked child riding on a horse as happiness and joy abound. This child is naked because he has nothing left to hide; nothing is holding him back. He is childlike again. The Sun is shining upon you now. Enjoy your life, celebrate, and be happy. You are in a good place; enjoy it while it is here. Embrace your individuality. Receiving the Sun card is a big yes in your life. Open your heart, embrace the Sun's energy, and be free. It is time for success!

Energies of the Sun

- happiness
- freedom
- childlike energy
- success
- joy

The Sun's Essential Oil: Sweet Orange Oil
ELEMENT: Fire
PLANETARY INFLUENCE: Sun
SCENT DESCRIPTION: Oh, the scent of orange: it
    is a bright, joyous, and uplifting scent, citrusy and
    sweet and just lovely!

I chose sweet orange oil because of its uplifting and joyous scent as well as its affinity to the Sun. We all know that the orange tree thrives in the sunlight. This oil is so happy and carefree, calling in the energies of success, emotional well-being, abundance, and a positive outlook on life. The orange tree is the only plant that creates three different essential oils: one from the flowers of the tree (neroli), one from the fruit itself (the orange), and one from the leaves and twigs of the plant (petitgrain). All of these oils foster happiness of some sort. Neroli fosters love, happy relationships, beauty, and inner well-being. Petitgrain fosters self-confidence and the ability to reach for what is needed in life. The fruit of the tree, the orange, is pure joy and happiness, peace, love, and success. Calling in the orange oils to support your joy during the energy of the Sun is the perfect magical influence.

CINNAMON ORANGE BLACK TEA

Use 1 teaspoon of a black tea of your choice. Add in a pinch of cinnamon and a pinch of dried orange peel. Be careful not to add too much dried orange peel as it can make your tea bitter. Blend together and put into a tea strainer. Add hot water and let brew for 3–5 minutes.

Downsides of the Sun

- ego

- arrogance

- failure

Support from the Council of Queens

Calling in the Queen of Wands could support the fire element energy that you already have going. Use this energy to be creative and powerful. Work magic with this queen while you are on fire. Celebrate your life by burning candles to give thanks to your guides and ancestors. This is a powerful time for you; share it. The Queen of Wands is very magical and is a wonderful source of charisma. Now is the time to use this magnetism to create new beginnings that can bring about the fruition of future goals.

The Queen of Pentacles can help you create success and happiness in the foundation of your life. She can help you plant and grow your success.

The Queen of Swords can help you communicate your success or your message to the world. She can help you speak your truth as well as create order.

The Queen of Cups can help you be open to receive and truly embrace the joy, freedom, and success that has entered your life. Often when success or happiness comes into our lives, we have difficulty embracing it wholeheartedly. The Queen of Cups will open your heart and allow these feelings to flow through you, therefore not allowing them to escape your attention. In this manner you will be truly grateful.

Companion Cards

The Sun is number 19 in the tarot. Here you can reduce the number 19, $1 + 9 = 10$, to call in the energy of the Wheel of Fortune, and then you can reduce the number 10 through $1 + 0 = 1$ to the Magician. You can work with the power of change with the Wheel of Fortune, allowing you to use your individuality and personal charisma to call in success and create the changes you want to see happen. You can call in the power of manifestation with the Magician. Manifest the changes you wish to see in your life. With the power of the Sun behind you, you have everything you need.

Judgment

NUMBER: 20
ELEMENT: Fire, water
PLANETARY INFLUENCE: Pluto

A Message from Judgment

I am Judgment, and I bring the gift of sound. Archangel Gabriel often sits on this card, blowing the horn of awareness. Are you hearing the call? I offer a transformation, an opportunity to find new direction, possibly your life purpose. Hear me, for I speak to you. Who you were before is not who you are now. You have grown and become aware of your true being. Lift your head up to the sound of the trumpeter and walk freely into your new world.

Meanings

If you have chosen Judgment or Judgment has chosen you, now is a time of rebirth. Everything is new. You are free and open to receive again. Are you hearing the call? Can you feel the shift coming? There is a new soul awareness happening within, and clarity abounds. In a sense, this is a review of one's life up to this point in time, allowing for a judgment to be made. Through this judgment a friendship must be made with the past, allowing for new freedom from limitation. Through this self-examination comes the sound of the trumpet calling for a new direction or one's life purpose. Again, as with the Sun card, there is nothing left to hide; all has been seen, and the path is lit before you.

Energies of Judgment

■ rebirth

■ hearing the call

- awakening

- aha moment

- freedom

Judgment's Essential Oil: Myrrh

ELEMENT: Water

PLANETARY INFLUENCE: Pluto

SCENT DESCRIPTION: Rich and calming, with a spicy and resinous quality.

I chose myrrh because of its relationship to Pluto as well as its relationship to spirituality. Myrrh comes from the resin of the *Commiphora*, which is a small thorny and shrubby tree native to northeastern Africa and the Red Sea region. The resin of the tree drips from the plant in order to heal the tree. This resin also helps heal us. Myrrh is healing, physically purifying, and carries the energy of spirituality. During the energy of Judgment, we are reborn. Myrrh essential oil can help to purify, heal, and release blockages, as well as help clear the aura. This allows for the opening of the spirit as well as thought and mind. Myrrh has always been a sacred oil used in purification rituals for the living as well as the dead. As we rise up in rebirth, work with myrrh essential oil to cleanse and heal the soul, allowing for peace within the heart, mind, and spirit.

Downsides of Judgment

- fear of change

- stagnation

- being judgmental

- fear of allowing self to become (not listening to the call)

Support from the Council of Queens

The Queen of Pentacles will help you ground and take the next step forward in this new time of being. She will allow for growth and security as a new era begins through rooting, therefore allowing you to reach for new heights. Here you can stand firm as all else around you may be changing.

The Queen of Swords can help with inspiration as well as logical movement forward. She can bring clarity and truth to your core allowing you to move forward with the spirit of adventure. The Queen of Swords will guide you through any new movement as well as help one to listen to the call with inspired clarity.

The Queen of Wands can stimulate your passions and your magic for your new adventure. She can help you to create. The Queen of Wands can also help you through your transformation through the act of shedding your skin. She will help to create your cauldron of Fire to call in the magic, power, and strength to move forward in your desired direction.

The Queen of Cups can help with the purification and healing of the new you. She will help to release unhealthy and restricting energies as well as to release emotional blockages. She will support your emotional growth and increase your intuition.

Companion Cards

The companion cards for Judgment (20) are the High Priestess $(2+0=2)$ and Justice $(1+1=2)$. The High Priestess will support your intuition during this time. She will help call in your inner council as you move to new beginnings and the rebirth of you. Justice can help balance the new energies around you as well as create order and clarity for movement forward. Justice will support order and control for a new foundation to form. During this time of rebirth, finding a new balance is essential.

The World

NUMBER: 21

ELEMENT: Earth

PLANETARY INFLUENCE: Saturn

A Message from the World

I am the World, and I am here to congratulate you. Look where you are standing and look at what you have accomplished. You have pulled together all that you are and now see yourself as whole. The merging together of your inner world and your outer being is complete, and what you have set out to accomplish is here now before you. Celebrate your success and stand tall in who you are, for as this cycle is now complete, a new beginning is before you as the world turns.

Meanings

If you have chosen the World or the World has chosen you, it is time to celebrate! The World card states that you have accomplished your goals; you stand in the center of the world in all your glory. You have heard the call and you now stand in your truth of who you are. This is a yes card in that it is giving you all that you have been striving for. You are now united with all that surrounds you as well as all that is within you. This is a card of all energies coming together to support your growth. All four elements are on this card to choose from to help call in your support and success. You are open to receive as well as give. This card is about limitless possibilities, yet it is ruled by Saturn, which is a planet of boundaries and limitations. We are all limited by the boundaries of the earth. This card represents the freedom from our own self-imposed limitations that allows for success. Enjoy the abundance of this time and be free.

Revel in the glory now, for the earth turns and new beginnings are just around the corner.

Energies of the World

- success
- completion
- abundance
- wholeness
- new beginnings
- masterpiece
- contentment

The World's Essential Oil: Australian Sandalwood
ELEMENT: Earth, air, water
PLANETARY INFLUENCE: Mercury, Moon, Venus
SCENT DESCRIPTION: Sandalwood has a light, uplifting, woody scent.

I chose Australian sandalwood because of its sweet and earthy quality. I love the light woody scent. This oil is uplifting, calming, and deep. The World card has all four elements available for use, just like in the Magician card. Sandalwood carries the energies of three of the four elements. Sandalwood also relates to Venus, which is the planetary influence for the Empress, which is the companion card for the World (think $2 + 1 = 3$). Sandalwood supports grounding energy, abundance, growth, strength, and vitality: all earth element qualities.

Sandalwood supports clarity of thought as well as inspiration, all qualities of air. When I breathe in the scent of sandalwood, I feel uplifted and close to my guides, angels, and ancestors. At the same time I feel as if I am walking through a wooded forest with the sun shining through and hitting the wood of the trees, enhancing the warm scent. As sandalwood brings a sense of well-being and healing within, here we find the qualities of the water element. Sandalwood is a well-rounded oil that calls in the energies of the elements for support, grounding, inspiration, healing, and well-being.

Downsides of the World

- limitation
- delay
- unresolved energy
- lack of clarity (unable to hear the call)

Support from the Council of Queens

I believe you could call in any of the queens with the World card. It all depends on what you are working on and which energies you really require for guidance and assistance. Call on the Queen of Pentacles for abundance, more growth, and grounding, and the Queen of Cups for flow and intuition as well as spiritual trust, healing, and connection. The Queen of Wands supports magic, charisma, creativity, and strength, and the Queen of Swords assists clarity, inspiration, and communication.

Companion Cards

The companion cards for the World (21) are the Empress (2 + 1 = 3) and the Hanged Man (1 + 2 = 3). You have reached a magical point in your life. You have success and have landed right where you wanted to be. What is next? You can call in the Empress for growth, abundance, fertility, and nurturing energy. The Empress can help you continue to reach for more. As you create and expand upon what you have already created, you also create a new foundation for the Fool to land upon as you start again.

The Hanged Man can be called in to help you surrender to the call and allow yourself to move with the flow of change. He will help you release what needs to be washed away, as well as connect to the spirit and possibly find a new perspective for your movement forward.

3

The Power of Numerology

In the tarot apothecary approach, numerology is key to self-discovery. There are several components to your numerology, the first being who you are in the tarot. This number or combination of numbers is based off your birth date and tells you about your personality as well as who you came on this earth to be. In this number or combination of numbers, you discover your gifts and challenges for this lifetime. This can help you determine your career and lifetime goals and create your path forward.

The next aspect of your numerology is based off the current year's energy. This numerology is derived from adding together your birth month + your birthday + the current year. This information gives you the gifts and challenges of your current year and allows you to embrace the gifts of the year and be aware of the challenges you may face so that you are equipped with the tools and knowledge needed to create the most productive and powerful year to your advantage.

Your numerology can also tell you about your shadow side, or what is hidden in your personality that you may be unaware of. This information allows you to become aware of these aspects of yourself that are hidden, therefore giving you the power to work through these challenges and create a more powerful you.

In this chapter we will discuss all of the numerology combinations so that you can gain a greater knowledge of who you truly are and therefore gather more insight to the power you carry in this lifetime.

Your Birth Cards

I will never forget the day I discovered Mary K. Greer's book *Who Are You in the Tarot?* This was about ten years ago on a used bookstore shelf. My husband and I were on vacation at the beach. We love used bookstores. If there is a used bookstore in the town we are visiting, we are there. This was back when Greer's book was called *Tarot Constellations*, and I really had no idea what it was about, so I bought it. It is one of the best buys I have ever made.

I basically live my life by this book. Once I discovered my numerology and who I was in the tarot, I felt like I finally understood myself. Using Greer's formula in the book, I am the Hermit and the Moon. My whole life I could never really figure out who I wanted to be and what my purpose was. Everyone in my family seemed to know who they were and where they were going, but not me. I received a college degree in music performance with a minor in business. I had no idea what to do with any of this. I just knew that I liked to sing and I liked to perform. I ended up working in the medical field after college because that is what opened up for me and I took it. It was not what I truly wanted, but it gave me the opportunity to work with people and I liked that. I was never truly happy in this field of work but I just kept going, searching for something new. When I discovered I was the Hermit and the Moon, my path became clear to me.

Because I am the Hermit, my path is lit by that of the Moon and the lantern, not the Sun. I did not need to know who I was at this point in life, I just needed to trust in my intuition, my inner guide to lead the way, and I would get there. One day I would look back at my life and gather all the treasures I had picked up along the road, and these treasures and gifts would point the way. I believe I have now found my direction, my way, and who I am. As the Hermit, I am a teacher and a guide for others, and this is who I have now become.

I have found that the discovery of who you are in the tarot can change your life. Understanding and knowing your personal skills, challenges, and gifts not only points you in a new direction, but this knowledge reinforces and confirms your desire to become who you know you truly are. This knowledge calls in the energy of courage, strength, trust, and belief in self. This allows you to move forward with a newfound trust in who you are and what you can accomplish in this life.

Calculating Your Personal Numerology

Calculating your numerology is simple. All you need to do is add together your birth date. Say that your birthday is October 4, 1919. In this case, you would add together $10 + 4 + 1919 = 1933$. Then you add together $1 + 9 + 3 + 3 = 16$. Then reduce the 16 down to 7: $1 + 6 = 7$. It's that simple.

For the tarot apothecary approach, your numerology is based on the major arcana in the tarot. There are twenty-two major arcana cards to work with. In the case just mentioned above, number 16 in the tarot is the Tower card, and when you reduce 16 down to 7, you have the Chariot. So our example person with this birth date of 10/4/1919 would be both the Chariot and the Tower.

Here is a list of the major arcana with their corresponding numbers; in tarot often the majors are numbered using roman numerals, which are listed here after the names:

0/22	Fool	0
1	Magician	I
2	High Priestess	II
3	Empress	III
4	Emperor	IV
5	Hierophant	V
6	Lovers	VI
7	Chariot	VII
8	Strength	VIII
9	Hermit	IX
10	Wheel of Fortune	X
11	Justice	XI
12	Hanged Man	XII
13	Death	XIII
14	Temperance	XIV
15	Devil	XV
16	Tower	XVI
17	Star	XVII
18	Moon	XVIII
19	Sun	XIX
20	Judgment	XX
21	World	XXI

There are different categories of cards within this system that further define their meaning: the personality card (highest number), teacher card (only for those whose top number is 19; more on this below), hidden factor card (middle number), and soul card (lowest number). In our example, then, with the numbers 16/7, the Chariot is the soul card (7) and the Tower is the personality card (16). Sometimes the numerology will reduce down to a single digit. If this is the case, this individual's soul and personality cards would be the same.

Personality Card
the highest number in the combination

The personality card speaks of how you show yourself in the world. How do others see you? What gifts does your personality bring, and what challenges need to be worked through in this lifetime?

Teacher Card
only for 19/10/1 combination

If your top number adds up to the number 19, then your combination will have three numbers in it: $1 + 9 = 10$, and $1 + 0 = 1$; you would be a 19/10/1. This is the only combination that will have three numbers in its numerology and the only combination to have a teacher card. In this combination, the Wheel of Fortune (10) is the teacher card. Here you learn about change and how to embrace its energies. You will learn about flexibility, adjusting, and the ability to see and grab on to opportunity. This individual has the Magician (number 1) as their soul card and the Sun (number 19) as their personality card.

This middle card in the combination, 10, represents lessons that may need to be worked with and learned along the life path. This individual will need to learn from and embrace the energies of the Wheel of Fortune when needed.

Hidden Factor Card
the hidden number in the combination

In some cases there is what Greer calls the "hidden factor" card. The hidden factor card is a shadow card. This is an energy that may surface off and on in an individual's life to help teach and bring forward challenges and obstacles that need to be worked through, understood, and surmounted in order to gain needed knowledge and move forward. The hidden factor card is hidden in all numbers 22 or below that would also reduce to the lowest form of the number combination.

For example, let us take a look at an individual who is a 21/3. This individual would have the Empress (3) as a soul card and the World (21) as a personality card. To find the hidden number for 21/3, we want to see if there are any other numbers between 1 and 22 that also reduce down to 3; the number 12 also reduces down to 3 $(1 + 2 = 3)$. Although this number did not show up in the numerology, it is still a factor of the individual's numerological makeup. It is hidden. The number 12 in the tarot is the Hanged Man. So this individual would want to study the energies of the Hanged Man as well as those of the World and the Empress. The Hanged Man is a shadow side to this individual since it is hidden in the numerology. All of these cards play a part in the life of this individual.

Soul Card
the lowest number in the combination

The soul card speaks of who you came into this life to become. What is your purpose here on this planet? What are the skills you have been given for this lifetime, and where can these skills lead you? What can you accomplish in this lifetime? What are your challenges?

■ ■ ■ ■

All other combinations are one- or two-card combinations, meaning that your number may reduce down to a single digit or be two numbers, such as a 17/8 or an 18/9. In any case, you will want to look at your highest number in your numerology and reduce it down to the lowest number possible. All of the numbers in your personal numerology that are between 1 and 22 will play some part in your life's journey.

Now in some cases, if a number adds up to anything above the number 22, such as 23, you would add together 2 + 3 = 5. This individual's personality and soul cards are represented by the number 5. Here you find a single-digit combination. The fifth card in the major arcana is the Hierophant. In this combination we have the hidden factor of 14 (1 + 4 = 5), Temperance, which can be added together to equal the number 5.

Since the Fool in the tarot is number 0, this approach designates the Fool as number 22 so that you can work with the card in a numerological manner. Some folks may be a 22/4, meaning they are the Fool (22) and the Emperor (4). The number 13 also adds up to 4 (1 + 3), setting the Death card as a hidden factor for the 22/4 individual.

Double Numbers

Now let's take a moment to discuss double numbers and their meanings. We will only be looking at numbers 10–22 since these are the double numbers associated with the major arcana. In the case of double numbers, the Fool can be number 22 and 0, so the Fool can show up in the number 10 as the second digit in the number, the 0, as well as the total number of 22. According to master numerologist Hans Decoz, double numbers still truly hold the energy of their root number. For example, let's look at the 16/7 combination of the Tower and the Chariot. In this combination we are truly striving to step into and embrace the energy of the Chariot, number 7. When working with double numbers, we want to look at the power of each digit individually, so in the 16/7 combination we have the power of the number 1, the number 6, and the number 7.

Remember that the root number is our soul card and the double number is our personality. Sometimes our personality is advantageous to our situation and sometimes it can be a hindrance.

Sometimes we have challenges in our personality that we need to work through in this lifetime. So this individual is working through the power of the number 16 as their personality in this lifetime. They are harnessing the power of number 6 and the number 1 to create the reality of the number 7. So in this combination we find possible struggles with relationships and choice indicated by the Lovers (6) and possible struggles with the ego, the self, and confidence or lack thereof in the Magician (1). You can see how the Tower (16) may crumble under lack of confidence or the ego being out of control. The Tower also may crumble when we do not make good choices, when we follow the ego instead of the heart, or when we let relationships bind us and hold us back. This is Tower time. So this individual will need to work with relationships and learn from them, as well as learn to have a clear and positive self-image. This individual will also need to work through the energy of change. We also have the positive powers of each number to embrace: the Magician (1) for creating self upon the earth and the Lovers (6) for creating relationships and choices that best suit our path. Let's not forget that we have the number 7 for movement forward.

Another example would be 21/3 and 12/3. Here we have both combinations striving to accomplish the energy of the Empress, number 3, in this lifetime, yet we find that these two personalities are different and may accomplish their goals and have challenges in different ways due to their double number personality. The 21/3 is working with the Magician (1) through the energy of the High Priestess (2) to create growth through the Empress (3). In this combination we have the Magician (1) working with the powers of the 2, harnessing the power of the High Priestess, to create growth as the Empress. The Magician energy is solid, and he is harnessing the power of the 2 to create his magic upon the earth.

On the other hand, in the combination of the 12/3 we have the High Priestess (2) working with the Magician (1) to manifest expressive growth as the Empress. In this combination the individual is still learning to trust their intuition, their higher self, through letting go, surrendering to what is, and beginning to understand and accept their knowing. Here the Magician is still learning about himself through listening to his intuition and beginning to trust himself. In the 21/3 combination of the World (21) and the Empress (3), the Magician is more established and is using his powers, where the 12/3 combination of the Hanged Man (12) and the Empress (3) is learning through this lifetime to trust their intuition in order to create what they desire upon the earth.

Another example is the Moon (18) and the Hermit (9), the 18/9. This combination is working with Strength (8) to help develop their Magician (1) self-power. This will help to trust and develop their intuition and self-knowing in order to become a guide and teach others through the life path of the Hermit. The Hermit must have strength to take his life journey of self-discovery and knowing. He must have strength to walk through the dark of the Moon. The 18/9 has the power and challenges of the Magician (1) and Strength (8). This individual would want to work with and understand the energies of the Magician, Strength, the Hermit, and the Moon in this lifetime. Through the knowledge of both the number 1 and the number 8, the Hermit develops the self-trust and knowledge to lead others on their path.

The key to working with the double numbers is to remember that the second digit in the double number combination is working through the energy of the first digit to create the base number. So 17/8 is working with the number 7 (Chariot) for movement forward through trials of the self, number 1 (Magician) to create the Strength (8) needed to become and create the powerful, courageous human being that this individual wishes to manifest as upon the earth. The Star (17) creates the hope and inspiration to continue to move forward in life. This creates the Strength (8) needed to manifest the power of you. This individual will need to tap into the power of hope in their lifetime in order to find their own personal strength. At times in their life, they will need to depend on their own inspiration for courage and movement forward on their path.

There is so much more to numerology to discover, but for purposes for understanding and working with the tarot apothecary, I believe that this is enough information to create a solid foundation. Study each number in your tarot numerology combination. What are the powers of these numbers, which tarot cards relate, and what can these cards gift you? What challenges need to be surmounted? This is powerful information that can help guide you through energy challenges and help harness your personal powers.

Once you have calculated and discovered your personal archetypes, then study those cards. What are the positive qualities of this archetype? What are the challenges for this archetype? How can you embody the desired qualities of this archetype to further your life? What do you know about this archetype that is true in your personal life?

This is the first step in your discovery. Who are you in the tarot? Understanding and working with this knowledge will help move you forward.

Some Tarot Numerology Combinations

Please note that not everyone will have a teacher card or a hidden factor card in their combination. Everyone will have a soul and a personality card. I have not listed all combinations here, but if you take a look at each number in your combination, as well as each major arcana card that relates to that number, you will begin to discover your personal gifts and challenges in this lifetime.

- The Magician: 1, 10, and 19

    19/10/1 = Sun (19) as a personality card, Wheel of Fortune (10) as a teacher card, Magician (1) as the soul card.

    10/1 = Wheel of Fortune (10) as a personality card, Magician (1) as a soul card, Sun as a hidden factor card.

- The High Priestess: 2, 11, and 20

    20/2 = Judgment as a personality card, the High Priestess as a soul card, Justice as a hidden factor card.

    11/2 = Justice as a personality card, the High Priestess as a soul card, Judgment as a hidden factor card.

- The Empress: 3, 12, and 21

    21/3 = the World as a personality card, the Empress as a soul card, the Hanged Man as a hidden factor card.

    12/3 = the Hanged Man as a personality card, the Empress as a soul card, the World as a hidden factor card.

- The Emperor: 4, 13, and 22

    22/4 = the Fool as a personality card, the Emperor as a soul card, Death as a hidden factor card.

    13/4 = Death as a personality card, the Emperor as a soul card, the Fool as a hidden factor card.

- The Hierophant: 5 and 14

    14/5 = Temperance as a personality card, the Hierophant as a soul card.

    5 = the Hierophant as a personality and soul card, Temperance as a hidden factor card.

- The Lovers: 6 and 15

    15/6 = the Devil as a personality card, the Lovers as a soul card.

    6 = the Lovers as a personality and soul card, the Devil as a hidden factor card.

- The Chariot: 7 and 16

    16/7 = the Tower as a personality card, the Chariot as a soul card.

    7 = the Chariot as a personality and soul card, the Tower as a hidden factor card.

- Strength: 8 and 17

    17/8 = the Star as a personality card, Strength as a soul card.

    8 = Strength as a personality and soul card, the Star as a hidden factor card.

- The Hermit: 9 and 18

    18/9 = Moon as a personality card, Hermit as a soul card.

    9 = Hermit as a personality and soul card, Moon as a hidden factor card.

■ ■ ■ ■

As you can see, there is power in numerology. Numerology can show you who you stepped into this lifetime as and who you can become. Numerology reinforces the power of your skills as well as what your challenges are in this lifetime and how you can be of service to yourself as well as the whole world. Numerology allows you to be courageous, with confidence in your truth and your ability to create your best, most powerful self.

Your Year Card

My favorite way to work with the tarot apothecary approach is to calculate and embrace my yearly tarot energy. For example, if your birthday is 10/4/1919 and we are currently in the year 2020, you would add together $10 + 4 + 2020 = 2034$, then add $2 + 0 + 3 + 4 = 9$. This individual would be in their Hermit year, number nine in the major arcana, and therefore would work with Hermit energy throughout the year.

Using the above example, if you have *not* had your birthday in the year of 2020 as of yet, you would add together $10 + 4 + 2019 = 8$, meaning you would be in a Strength year until your birthday in 2020. Let's say it is now March of the year 2020 and your birthday is not until December 8, 2020; then your calculation would be $12 + 8 + 2019$. This is because you have not experienced your birth date in the current year. On December 8, 2020, you enter into a new tarot year and would now use the calculation of $12 + 8 + 2020 = 2040$. Add together $2 + 0 + 4 + 0 = 6$. This would be your Lovers year, which is number 6 in the major arcana.

When working with your year card, you do not want to reduce down to the lowest number if your number falls between 1 and 22. These are the numbers of the major arcana and we will embrace many of these energies throughout our lifetimes. So if your numerology adds up to 18, then the Moon, number 18 in the tarot, would be your yearly energy.

When working with a tarot year, you have the opportunity to call in support from another card if you wish. Look at your numerology. Let's say you are currently in your Moon year, number 18. The Moon's energy can be intense, so you can reduce the 18 down to 9 if you like and call in the Hermit number 9 for wisdom and grounding through your journey in your Moon year. The Hermit is the companion card for the Moon since it fits into the Moon's numerology, as in $1 + 8 = 9$. You are still in your Moon year, yet you are asking for support from the Hermit to help you to have a successful Moon year. You can also choose to call in any card you like for support—maybe a queen or any other major arcana card you desire to help support your movement forward.

Working with the year card has been the most powerful tool I have ever used. In this manner you will understand the energy of the year that you are stepping into and therefore be more prepared for that year and be able to make clear decisions based on that year's energy. Let's say you are currently in your Hierophant year. The Hierophant year generally leads to study of some sort, higher education, or spirituality and tradition. Maybe you will go back to school during this year or join a spiritual community. I generally find myself taking a course of some sort during this time and calling in new knowledge. During my last Hierophant year, I went to herbalism school.

Another example: As I stepped into my Lovers year, a year relating to relationships and choice, everything changed for me. My birthday was in the beginning of March. By April 3 I was laid off from my job due to COVID-19, so those employee relationships went away. This opened up the opportunity for me to write this book. Through this process I have created many new relationships through my writing community.

My big choice came when I was offered a business opportunity that in time could bring in a great financial flow. This opportunity would take some time to lay a foundation and would require that I put in a lot of work immediately. If I decided to take this business opportunity, I would not have time to write the book. It was a tough decision. I was taught by my parents to be responsible and take the opportunity that would call in financial flow and a solid foundation. I cried for days on this decision. I remembered that with the energy of the Lovers, it is important to listen to and follow the heart, so I did just that. I finally gathered up my courage and said no to the offer.

Today I am on a new path. The interesting thing is that when I stepped into my Lovers year, I decided that I wanted to also work with the Fool energy. Even though the Fool is not part of my numerology for the year, I wanted to embrace the energy of freedom and new beginnings. I knew I was at a crossroads, and I knew I was now sixty and ready for change. I really did not want to go backward in my life. It was time to embrace a new beginning. I chose to take the leap of faith before I even knew what I would be jumping into. I jumped—and here I am: a writer, a teacher, and a potion maker. I embraced my Lovers year and called in support from the Fool.

I also wanted to call in plant energy support in my Lovers year, so I chose lavender. I was really attracted to lavender and since it's an essential oil that corresponds to the air element—as do the Fool and the Lovers cards—it would be a perfect fit. During this time I also became attracted to the stone lapis lazuli and bought lapis jewelry for my adventure. Once again, it's related to the air element. Another tool I picked up was the flower essence of walnut for accepting change in my life and lots of mint and dandelion tea for the Fool's energy of freedom. So far, I am on my way and feeling great about it.

As you can see, tarot numerology is a powerful way to work with the energies that are entering into your life. Are you in your Tower year? Maybe you need some grounding for support, so why not ask the Queen of Pentacles to come in? Are you in the Chariot year and need to charge forward with focused intention and not allow your emotions to persuade you differently? Work with a water element oil such as lemon balm to calm your emotions or an air element oil such as rosemary for clarity and focus along the way. Call in support and walk through your year with more courage, strength, determination, and resolve. Allow yourself to really experience the year and learn the year's message. You will feel powerful throughout your journey and walk through the year with a more determined direction. You will walk closer to your desires when you learn to embrace the energies surrounding you and harness the power of your tarot year.

Not everyone will experience every tarot year in their lifetime. As Greer states in *Who Are You in the Tarot*, no one will experience the Magician as a personality/soul card, hidden factor card, or year card in this era. The High Priestess will only be experienced by a few as a year card and will only appear as a year card once in those few people's life. There will be no more High Priestess years after January 1, 1998, through December 31, 9958.

I personally calculated my year cards back to the day I was born and into my eighties, and I never experience the Tower or the Star. This is why calling in the energies of these cards when you need their support is of importance. Since I don't experience the energy of the Tower in my lifetime, I may need to embrace the energy of the Tower from time to time in order to learn to allow some things in my life to fall away and let go of what is not serving me. Maybe I need to learn to accept when life suddenly changes without notice— to learn to walk through chaos. The Star can teach me to have hope and be grateful for times of well-being in my life.

When combined with the tarot majors, personal numerology becomes a very powerful and personal tool. You will gain a better understanding of who you are and where you are going. You will call in the support of the plant kingdom and walk your path with determination and a better understanding of life lessons. Through walking through the journey of the tarot, you gain the knowledge and skills needed for success. Now that you know who you are in the tarot and what your current year is, you can now set an intention for your movement forward.

Goal Setting with Your Birth and Year Cards

Once you have determined who you are in the tarot and what year you are currently in, you have a better view of what energies may surface during the current year and how you will possibly work with and react to those energies. You are better able to chart your path forward. Your personal numerology tells you who you are, what skills and talents you have, and what challenges cloak your life. How might you best share your personal energy with the world? Are you on your desired path or is there a deep-seated desire to step out on a new path? Is this new path in alignment with your skills and personal energies? How can you use the attributes of your archetype to grasp onto and empower yourself to accomplish your goals? The year you are in within the tarot tells you what energies are entering your space and what types of challenges may lie ahead of you as well as what key powers may be available for your use. Let's take a look at an example.

Let's say I am working with a friend who is a clinical social worker and has a very full and grounded practice in counseling. This individual is deeply rooted into the rules and regulations of the system, yet she has a desire to incorporate her spiritual side into the equation. She personally works with tarot and oracle cards, but she feels somewhat restricted and personally held back from allowing these tools into her practice due to the box she has been put into through the system. She feels fearful of letting her true, authentic nature surface and be seen by the world, and she is not sure she wants to open up this side of herself to the counseling community as a whole. After looking into her personal numerology, we find that her birth card in the tarot is the Lovers. This makes perfect sense. This situation is in alignment with her Lovers energies of working with relationships, first learning from personal relationships and then taking that knowledge into her practice as a counselor. She has found her path, yet she has this desire to counsel others through the use of spiritual tools such as tarot and oracle cards. This would allow her to be her true, authentic self.

When looking into the current year's energy for this friend, we find that she is now in her Chariot year. This is a year of movement forward with focused intention. One can accomplish a great deal during this year if they have chosen a direction in which to focus. After talking with my friend and discussing her year ahead, she mentioned that she has found a new passion in working with Photoshop. She has been creating magical images and writing about them. Through this process of learning, an idea appeared to her. Maybe she could create her own oracle deck and start a new way of reaching out into the world. This may not be how she works in the clinical world, but if she was to create an oracle deck she could also reach others and be of support in the spiritual manner she is looking for. This is a new discovery and a possible path forward. She can now choose to focus her intention on creating her deck and charting the Chariot year forward toward her goal.

Let's say this same friend is in her Hermit year instead of the Chariot. A Hermit year would be a time of self-contemplation and searching within for her answers. This may not be a time of charging forward but more of a time to reach within to discover her oracle deck and spend her time in communion with her idea. Maybe she does not create the deck during this year but spends her time reaching within for the discovery of her images and keywords for her deck. More than likely she will start creating and sending the deck out into the world in the following year, her Wheel of Fortune year, a year of change and fortune.

As you can see, your tarot year really is a powerful way to take the next step on your path by embracing and working with that year's energy. What qualities does this archetype offer and how can you use these qualities to your advantage? Make a list of the powers and challenges of the year and create your magic.

THE POWER OF NUMEROLOGY

Chart your path forward by first discovering who you are in the tarot (your soul card). What does this tell you about your life right now? Are you on the path you would like to be on or is there a new direction in which you would like to move toward? What are your skills, and how can you put your best foot forward? Now calculate what year you are in within the tarot. What are the attributes and challenges of that year? How can you work with the energies of that year to advance on your path? Write down the keywords for the current year's archetype (you will find the description of each archetype along with their keywords in chapter 2) and use those words to empower yourself and help to make decisions throughout the year.

Is there another archetype along with your current year's archetype that you would like to call in for support? In the example above of my friend in her Chariot year, she has chosen to move forward and create her oracle deck. She is going to use the Chariot energy to keep focused on her goal and move toward its destination. The Chariot year asks you to not let your emotions and outside distractions get in the way of your desired destination. This can come about in the form of reactions to outside stimuli or possibly self-doubt and negative talk such as "Your art is not good enough; who would want to buy your work? Just forget about it and stay in your lane." Here we find emotional self-sabotage. In this case maybe she would possibly want to work with the Queen of Swords for clarity of thought and focus, therefore not allowing herself to be swayed by emotion. The Queen of Swords is the least emotional of the queens. Possibly she may choose the Empress to ground during her journey forward, allowing her to stay rooted in the project and call on her skills for beauty and aesthetics for the deck, as well as abundance and growth. Choosing a second archetype to work with is your choice: it is not a requirement.

At this point, you know who you are in the tarot as well as what year you are currently in. Now what qualities from your personal life archetype can you embrace? What qualities from your current year's energies can you use to your advantage? What challenges may arise due to these energies?

You have now gathered a lot of information on your journey of self-discovery, and more wisdom is just around the corner. A special journal is a great way to keep track of your growth through this process and chart your plans for movement forward. I recommend finding a journal that speaks to your dreams through color or artwork, as this will continue to inspire you on your journey.

Now for the next question: What is your intention for the year?

Intention and Imagination

Intention and imagination are key to finding success. What energies are you wanting to shift and what is your desired outcome? As Mary K. Greer suggests in *The Essence of Magic: Tarot, Ritual, and Aromatherapy*, imagination is key to magical success. You must envision the whole—the outcome, or the destination—before creating the detail. Once your desired intention is in place and you have a vision for what success looks like for you, then you can create a ritual or rituals to call in the desired energies.

Imagination allows you to create your vision, intention allows you to lay the foundation for movement forward, and ritual and spoken word create the magic behind the journey.

■ ■ ■ ■

You have now calculated your numerology. You know what energies lie ahead in the year. You have chosen your additional desired archetypal tarot energy that you wish to call in and work with. It is time to set your intention and allow your imagination to envision the whole. What does success truly look like for you? Spend some time in meditation and allow your imagination to take control. See your success and gather that vision into your magical cauldron; this is your will to become. What are the keywords for the year ahead that you wish to embrace? What elemental energies are you working with, and which simple everyday rituals speak to you within that elemental energy? Now is the time to create your ritual, mantra and altar. You are ready to do the magic; you are ready to create you. Throw your desires into your magical cauldron and stir. You are on your way.

I have created a self-discovery questionnaire below. You can now start to fill out this questionnaire for your personal discovery. As you will see, at this point in the book not everything in this questionnaire has been discussed, yet you do have the information of who you are in the tarot and what year you are currently in as well as your intention for movement forward for the year. You will be able to answer more questions on the questionnaire as you move forward in the book.

Self-Discovery Questionnaire

1. Who are you in the tarot?

Your birth card and w cards

- Add together your birth date here: birth month + birth day + birth year = (number)

- Example: birth date of June 12, 1974 = /
  $06 + 12 + 1974 = 1992 = 1 + 9 + 9 + 2 = 21 = 2 + 1 = 3$

- This individual's tarot card would be the Empress, with the World as her companion card.

- Who are you?

- Which of the personal qualities of your birth card do you wish to embrace right now in your life?

Major arcana cards for reference; you can write your keywords here.

0/22	Fool	_____
1	Magician	_____
2	High Priestess	_____
3	Empress	_____
4	Emperor	_____
5	Hierophant	_____
6	Lovers	_____
7	Chariot	_____
8	Strength	_____
9	Hermit	_____
10	Wheel of Fortune	_____
11	Justice	_____
12	Hanged Man	_____
13	Death	_____
14	Temperance	_____
15	Devil	_____
16	Tower	_____
17	Star	_____
18	Moon	_____
19	Sun	_____
20	Judgment	_____
21	World	_____

2. What year are you currently in the tarot?

Add together your birth month + birth day + the current year. If you have not had your birthday in the current year, then use the previous year here.

Example: birth date is December 12, 1984. Let's say the current date is October 1, 2020. Since you have not had your birthday in 2020 yet because your birthday is in December and it is currently October your calculation would be 12 + 12 + 2019. 12 + 12 + 2019 = 9, which would be the Hermit year. If you have already had your birthday in the current year then use the current year to calculate your number.

- What year are you in?
- What challenges does this year bring?
- What positive energies do you wish to embrace in this year?
- What elemental energy is your year card?
- Which essential oils relate to this card?
- Which crystals or stones relate?

3. What is your intention or goal right now?

- What challenges do you find regarding your intention or goal?

4. Is there another major arcana or queen archetype you wish to embrace right now? What qualities do you wish to embrace from this archetype?

Example: I am currently in my Chariot year and the energy of the Chariot is movement forward with a focused intention. If not focused, the horses on the card that represent duality can go in different directions therefore tearing you apart. Focus is key now. I have chosen to work with the Queen of Swords. She is focused and she is the least emotional queen. During this time I need to be focused and keep my emotions in check:

- What elemental energy is this archetype?
- Which essential oils are related to this element?
- Which crystals or stones relate?
- Which carrier oils will you use?
- Which colors relate to this archetype?

5. Blending Your Oil

Base Note: Plant Part: Scent Group:

Middle Note: Plant Part: Scent Group:

Top Note: Plant Part: Scent Group:

ADDITIONAL NOTES TO ADD

Plant Part: Scent Group:

Plant Part: Scent Group:

Plant Part: Scent Group:

6. Write a mantra for your intention and magical potion.

As an example, for an earth elemental mantra: "I am grounded. I am centered. I walk on solid ground, and that ground supports my growth. I have everything that I need and I create abundance in my life daily. I am truly blessed."

7. Which simple everyday rituals do you wish to incorporate?

Chapter References for Questions

- Who are you in the tarot? CHAPTER 3

- What year are you currently in? CHAPTER 3

- What is your intention for the year? CHAPTER 3

- What challenges does this year bring? CHAPTER 2 (study the archetype of your year card)

- What positive energies do you wish to embrace in this year? CHAPTER 2 (study the archetype of your year card)

- What elemental energy is your year card? CHAPTER 2 (study the archetype of your year card)

- Which essential oils relate to this card based on the elemental energy of the archetype? CHAPTER 4

- Which crystals or stones relate? CHAPTER 7

- Is there another archetypal energy you wish to call in for support this year? CHAPTER 2

- Choose and create your oil or essential oil blend. CHAPTER 6

- Write your mantra for movement forward. CHAPTER 8

- What rituals do you wish to embrace and work with this year? CHAPTER 9

■ ■ ■ ■

Now you have a starting point to move forward with.

4

Elemental Energies
and the Archetypes

Knowledge and understanding of the elemental energies that create our world and our being are extremely powerful tools to have under your belt. It wasn't until I understood how the elements work in and through everything that I began to understand tarot. The elements have been a large part of how humanity has viewed healing and understanding the energies within the body. For many centuries, this is all medicine knew. Many cultures have documented history with various systems relating to the elements and the medicines they worked with.

In Chinese medicine we find the elements of earth, water, metal (air), fire, and wood. In many belief systems in India we find the tattvas, a system of different energies of which five of the elements are a part of. In most Indian traditions there are more than five tattvas but the five elements stand strong in this system. India also brought us the medicinal tradition of Ayurveda. Ayurveda has quizzes you can take based on body type, and the physical energies that will set up what elements are your strongest. The elements are also worked with and valued in the traditions of the founding culture of the Americas, the Native Americans, as well as in Wicca, shamanism, and other magical traditions.

There is also a belief that each of us is made up of all four elements, but these elements are generally not in total balance. Finding an elemental balance helps bring about health and wellness. As you can see, there are many different traditions that work with and experience the elements in different ways. In some systems there are only four elements, and many have five or more. In the tarot apothecary approach, we will be working with the four elements of earth, water, fire, and air. There are four suits within the tarot structure, and each suit relates to one of the four elements. The suit of pentacles represents the earth element, cups represent water, wands represent fire, and swords represent air.

We will now take a look at each suit within the tarot and its elemental energy. Remember that the tarot apothecary approach does not work with an entire tarot deck. We work solely with the queens of each suit and the major arcana. As we look at each suit, we will also take a look at some essential oils that are a part of that suit's elemental energy.

Each major arcana card within the tarot also relates to a specific elemental energy, so we will discuss each major arcana card and its associations as well.

||||||||||||

> This chapter references some material that I will go more in-depth with in part 2. Chapter 5 will elaborate on essential oils and the parts of the plant they are created from. Chapter 6 will further define blending oils by note, scent group, and elemental energy.

Suit of Pentacles
EARTH ELEMENT

The suit of pentacles within tarot is an earth element suit. All of the cards within the minor arcana relating to the suit of pentacles, its royal court, and some major arcana cards relate to the earth element.

The earth element energy is about foundation, security, grounding, nourishment, structure, health, fertility, abundance, growth, making tangible, and nurturing. This suit is about matter and all we need to survive. Here we are working with food, home, family, job, money, work—all about creating our foundation for survival and success. Think Gaia, Mother Earth, who supports and supplies all we need to survive on the planet. In my mind's eye, I see vines reaching out for what they need and desire—the ability for growth and beauty. This is the earth element. The earth element is feminine energy, internal and seeking within. Earth is considered dry and cold. The earth can be dry and inflexible, crumbling at your feet. The cold relates to feminine energy and the desire to move inward.

The earth element relates to our bones, or physical structure, which supports us and allows for movement upon the earth. Earth also relates to the winter season, the midnight hour, and the direction north. Earth oils are derived from wood, bark, or the roots of the plant. These oils are derived from the parts of the plant that ground, nourish, balance, and support the plant's growth. Animals that relate to the earth element include bear, wolf, deer, ram, goat, hedgehog, boar, elephant, and caribou. My favorite earth animal is the polar bear because of how far north they live.

Characteristics of an Earth Individual

- strong in character
- dependable
- salt of the earth
- stubborn; stuck in the mud
- nurturing
- stable
- practical
- slow and steady
- resistant to change

Earth Element Careers

- nurse
- veterinarian
- mother
- farmer
- herbalist
- nanny
- artisan
- naturalistic doctor
- builder
- laborer
- banker
- financial adviser

Earth Astrology Signs

- Capricorn
- Taurus
- Virgo

Earth Cards

- Queen of Pentacles
- The Magician

  This card calls in the energy of channeling from above to help you create who you want to be upon this earth. A card of self-manifestation, this card has both earth and air elements. This is a very transformative card of creating tangible matter upon the earth.

- The Empress

  This card speaks of abundance, nurturing, growth, fertility, beauty, and grounding. The Empress is the combination of one and two, which creates growth. She brings all you need to survive and she nourishes you, calling in the energies of new ground.

- The Hierophant

  This card speaks of our higher authorities of education, religion, and traditions. Here we find the one who channels for others, the translator. We also find the church, spirituality, higher education, and community. This card is about conforming to or joining a form of structured community for self-development, whether that means going to school or joining a church we choose to be a part of. Are you a channel and translator for others? The Hierophant can also be asking you to seek spiritual or higher guidance.

- The Hermit

  The Hermit is our guide through life. This is the sage, the wise one, who has lived and experienced life and life's lessons and is now the guide for others to follow. The Hermit also asks that you look at what needs to be completed at this time in your life so that your path is clear to move forward. The Hermit helps you find your way on the path of life. Are you seeking a guide or are you the guide who is being sought after?

- The Devil

  The Devil is about our responsibility to ourselves and others. This card often asks "What are you bound to that is holding you back?" and "What are you attached to?" This card is also about enjoying the material aspects of life and having some fun while also being responsible. Break free and don't be attached to the outcome because attachment creates addiction. The keyword is responsibility.

- The World

  The World card represents our planet, Earth, so obviously it is earth element energy. This card speaks of success and finding one's way in the world. You have made it in life, so it's time to rejoice because the World turns. This card can also mean that you are on the right path and heading in the right direction.

Earth Essential Oils

Earthy oils often come from the wood or bark of a tree, the roots of the plant, and sometimes the resin of a tree. Resins such as benzoin have a deeper, darker scent to them. Frankincense has an almost earthy, woody scent. Sometimes the element is based off of where the essential oil was derived from and sometimes by the earthiness or darkness of the scent. You will also find herbaceous and spicy oils that are deep and dark in scent. If you think of the energy of roots and how they ground and support the plant nutritiously, you will see how they are earthy in nature. Tree wood and bark carry the energies of protection, security, and strength. They allow the plant to grow.

Earth oils give us many of the base note oils, which hold the blend down. They add support for growth and are generally longer-lasting scents. We will be looking at oils that are earthy in scent and hold the properties of grounding.

- Patchouli *(Pogostemon cablin)*

  Patchouli is a base note for blending. It is steam-distilled from the leaves of the plant and is part of the Lamiaceae family. Patchouli, otherwise known as "the hippie oil," is very deep and dark in scent and is part of the woody scent group. To me, patchouli smells like steak sauce on its own, but blended with other woody, herbaceous, floral, or spicy oils, it creates a deep foundation for a powerful scent.

- Vetiver *(Vetiveria zizanioides)*

  Vetiver is a base note for blending. Vetiver is steam-distilled from the roots of the plant, making it a powerful grounding oil. Vetiver is part of the Poaceae family. Vetiver is often used in the perfume industry as a fixative or grounding note for the blend (a fixative restricts the volatility of the fragrance and helps to prolong the longevity of the aroma; the grounding note is just the base note, or deepest scent). I absolutely love vetiver as it has a deep, dark, rich scent with a slight smoky undertone. Vetiver is a grass that is prevalent in India and Indonesia and is part of the woody scent group. It blends well with other woody oils as well as herbaceous, floral, and spicy scents.

- Benzoin *(Styrax benzoin)*

  Benzoin is a base or middle note. Benzoin is solvent-extracted from the gum of the tree. Benzoin is part of the Styracaceae family. This oil has a lovely scent: deep, sweet, and woody, with a vanilla aftertone. I blend with this oil often for its sweet vanilla tone. Although this essential oil is really a member of the water element, it is heavy enough to be used as a base note for its grounding effect. Benzoin is considered a water elemental oil because it is derived from the resin of the plant. Resins help to heal the wounds of the tree, therefore bringing in the element of water via healing energy. Resins are a more liquid form in their natural state although they can be thick and viscous. Benzoin blends well with other spicy oils as well as resinous, woody, and citrus oils.

- Amyris *(Amyris balsamifera)*

  Amyris is a base note for blending. Amyris is steam-distilled from the wood and bark of the tree. Amyris is part of the Rutaceae family. This oil has a wonderful scent that is very similar to sandalwood. It is in the woody scent group and blends well with other woody scents as well as herbaceous, spicy, and floral scents.

- Oakwood Absolute *(Quercus robur)*

  Oakwood absolute is a base note. It is solvent extracted from the wood of the tree. The mighty oak is part of the beech family. This oil is generally used in the perfume industry as a grounding/base note for perfumes. I love its deep, earthy, woody, and warming scent. It has a thicker physical form than most oils. This oil calls in the solidity of the mighty oak. Oakwood absolute is part of the woody scent group and blends well with other woody scents as well as herbaceous, spicy, and floral scents. I also associate oakwood with fire since oak trees stand taller than other trees and tend to hold more moisture, which makes them more vulnerable to lightning strikes.

- Angelica Root *(Angelica archangelica)*

  Angelica root is a middle to base note. Angelica root is extracted from the roots of the plant by steam distillation. There is another oil extracted from the seed of the Angelica plant that is listed in the fire oils. Angelica is part of the Apieceae family. Angelica root has a very interesting smell. The scent is very earthy with a herbaceous and medicinal tone to it. This oil is great for protection and is a great addition to any angelic and elemental magic. Angelica root is part of the herbaceous scent group and blends well with woody oils as well as herbaceous and citrus oils.

- Virginia Cedarwood *(Juniperus virginiana)*

  Cedarwood is a base to middle note for blending that is steam-distilled from the tree's wood. Cedar is a member of the Pinaceae family. Cedarwood has qualities in its scent and in its magical properties that relate it to all four elements: earth, water, fire, and air. Cedarwood has a deep, sweet, earthy scent that is very helpful with banishing and protecting. It is also a wonderful grounding oil. Cedarwood blends well with other woody scents in addition to herbaceous, spicy, and floral scents.

- Spanish Sage *(Salvia lavandulifolia)*

  Spanish sage is a middle note for blending that is steam-distilled from the plant's leaves. Sage is part of the Lamiaceae family. In the sage group you will also find common sage as well as clary sage. I never use common sage and most often use clary sage, which has more of a water elemental feel for me, so for earth elemental energies I use Spanish sage. Spanish sage has an herbaceous, minty, medicinal scent. Although sage carries the earth element energy, it also carries the energies of air due to the fact that sage is clearing and purifying when burned. Sage is a member of the herbaceous scent group and blends well with other herbaceous scents as well as with woody and citrus oils.

- Australian Sandalwood *(Santalum spicatum)*

Australian sandalwood is a base note for blending that is steam-distilled from the tree's roots and heartwood. Sandalwood is part of the Santalaceae family. This is another oil that carries the energy of more than one element. Here we find earth due to the fact that the oil is derived from the wood of the tree. We also find water and air elements in this oil. There is a calming energy to this oil, whose scent is woody, light, and airy yet deep, with a slight sweetness. This oil belongs to the woody scent group and blends well with other woody scents as well as herbaceous, spicy, and floral scents.

For other earth element oils, see the appendix.

Suit of Cups
WATER ELEMENT

The suit of cups within the tarot is a water element suit. All of the cards within the minor arcana that are a part of the suit of cups, the royal court, and some major arcana cards relate to the water element.

Water shows us the flow in life. We find emotions, feelings, love, community, relationship, joy, happiness, loss, grief, and fear. We also find healing and spirituality within the suit of cups. This suit calls in the use of intuition and mystery, the dark of the night, dream time, and psychic abilities.

The water element keeps things flowing in life. Internally it allows us to release emotions that may be causing blockages within our body and therefore allows for healing. We can also call in the water element to create a flow in our external life. When we feel stuck and unable to move forward, water can start things moving again and therefore break up stagnation.

Our first experience with water is within the womb. We are nurtured and cared for in the womb as we rest in water. The water element sits in the pelvic region of the body and relates to the second chakra. This is a very feminine energy that flows through us all. The image of the cup is open to receive, allowing for a flow of gifts, healing, and love.

Although water can be calming and peaceful, don't forget the power of water to destroy. Water energy is feminine, cold, and wet. The cold relates to feminine energy and the intention to move inward. Water also relates to the blood, sweat, and tears within our body as well as all the other bodily fluids such as urine and sexual fluids.

You will find that many of the essential oils that fall into the water category come from the flowers or the resin of a plant or tree, although there are floral scents that can come from other sources of the plant. Water's season is autumn, its time is twilight, and its direction is west.

Some animal guides for water include whale, dolphin, salmon, shark, sea turtle, octopus, crocodile, starfish, frog, and beaver. Think sea animals.

Characteristics of a Water Individual

- dreamy
- emotional
- can be wishy-washy
- intuitive
- healer
- escapist
- psychic
- sensitive
- sensual

- mysterious
- compassionate

Water Element Careers

- spiritual leader
- midwife
- healer
- musician
- mystic

Water Astrological Signs

- Cancer
- Scorpio
- Pisces

Water Cards

- Queen of Cups
- The High Priestess

  The High Priestess card is associated with intuition and the internal voice within. This card speaks of listening to your own voice and following the knowledge held within. The High Priestess is the one who knows. This card is not about movement but about the wisdom that lies in silence and stillness.

- The Chariot

  The Chariot is related to water because of its correspondence to the astrological sign of Cancer. The Chariot is about movement forward with intended focus in one direction. There is a large emphasis on emotional control with this card. Many tarot decks depict two horses or sphinxes charging forward on the Chariot card, one black and one white, representing duality. If emotions are out of control, therefore allowing for reaction to surrounding circumstances, one can lose focus and therefore lose control of the horses, causing total loss of the intended direction. Focus is the keyword for this card. If one is focused in a chosen direction, then a lot can be accomplished with the Chariot.

- The Hanged Man

  The Hanged Man is a very spiritual card asking for surrender to all that is. This card often shows a person hanging upside down, blindfolded, and gagged. This is a card of letting go and letting the universe guide the way. I often think of the Beatles' song "Let It Be." Since the man is hanging upside down, he now has to look at things with a different perspective, a different point of view. It is not about fighting the energies that be but finding a different way to look at the situation and allowing for a new vision. This card can feel as if you are wading in deep water, not going anywhere. The Hanged Man can feel as if there is a pause in your life and you are just treading water. However, throughout this time spirit is working within.

- Death

  As we are born from the womb of our mother, after being embraced in water, we die with the energy of water. Water is a form of purification allowing for transformation. Often Death is thought of as a dark and dreaded card to pull. In reality, Death is a card of releasing the dead wood of one's life so that new growth can emerge anew. This card is like being in the cocoon for a while and emerging as the butterfly. Death represents the removal of an aspect of our life that we no longer need. This card generally does not represent the death of a life form—more the death of an aspect of our self or life energy that was already dying and needed to break free.

- The Moon

  The Moon is a mysterious card—a card of the unknown. With the Moon, one's path is not lit by the light of the Moon because the moon only reflects light and cannot generate it. We must walk through the dark trusting only in our intuition and strength within. Often two hounds appear on the card. They represent fears we have. Once you walk through the fear, these hounds become your allies and companions. This card can represent the "dark night of the soul" or a time of unknown energies. Trust in yourself and search for the internal light within to guide the way. The path is not lit except through your self-trust, intuition, and courage. Through these gifts, the path becomes clear and your fears will subside. Step through this fear and find the cool waters of calm within. This card may just be telling you to listen within regarding the situation at hand.

- Temperance

  Temperance is a card of alchemy, taking two items and creating anew. Here is the blending of fire and water to create a new alchemical energy. We will discuss this card further with the fire element.

- Judgment

  Judgment is a card of rebirth. This is a journey of the soul into the cave of life with the emergence of a new being. Here I believe that both fire and water purify and transform. We will discuss this card further with the fire element.

Water Essential Oils

Water essential oils are sweet and healing and tend to be derived from flowers and resin. Think of how flowers attract pollinators. The water element is heart energy: love, joy, and compassion. Working with flower oils helps us call in and attract love and heart energy. The resin of a plant, such as a tree, helps heal that tree of any injuries to the bark, therefore calling in healing and protection. These resin oils help to heal and protect us as well. Water element energy is that of the heart, our feelings and emotions. In this way we can work with water element oils to open the heart to receive, attract love, and purify and heal our body and our spirit.

- Clary Sage *(Salvia sclarea)*

  Clary sage is a middle to base note. Clary sage is steam-distilled from the leaves and flowering tops of the plant. Although this oil is often associated with air element due to its connection to the sage plant, it can be associated with the water element due to its physical appearance. Clary sage has small silvery hairs on its leaves that tie this plant with the moon, thus calling in the water element. Clary sage has a somewhat sweet scent with a bit of earthiness and nuttiness to it. The word *clary* relates to the word *clarity*. The second half of the Latin name for this plant, *sclarea*, relates to the eye. Here we can translate those two words into "clear vision," which I associate with the High Priestess, who has the ability to look within and see all that is or ever has been. The word *sage* also relates to the wisdom of the High Priestess. Clary sage calls in the wisdom of the unknown and the wisdom that lies within the body (or self). Clary sage is part of the herbaceous scent group and blends well with other herbaceous scents as well as woody and citrus oils.

- Lemon Balm "Melissa" *(Melissa officinalis)*

    Lemon balm is a middle note. Melissa, aka lemon balm, is steam-distilled from the leaves and flowering tops of the plant. It is part of the Lamiaceae family. Lemon balm is often used in furniture polish and air fresheners. I remember the Daisy Air Freshener brand as a kid. My mom would plug them into the wall of the bathroom. It was in the shape of a daisy. In the center of the daisy was a bright yellow area that would emit a lemon balm scent when touched. Lemon balm has a lovely soft lemon scent. It is a calming and joyful oil. Lemon balm is a member of the citrus scent group and blends well with other citrus oils as well as with herbaceous, floral, and spicy scents.

- Roman Chamomile *(Chamaemelum nobilis)*
- German Chamomile *(Matricaria recutica)*

    There are two types of chamomile, Roman and German. Roman chamomile is a middle note, while German chamomile is a middle to base note. Both are steam-distilled from the flowering heads of the plant. Chamomile is a part of the Asteraceae family and is definitely a water element oil. Chamomile is very calming and peaceful, and is often drunk as a tea to help with sleep or upset stomach. Roman chamomile has a sweeter, lighter scent. German chamomile is blue in color and has a stronger yet still sweet and calming scent. Chamomile is part of the floral scent group and blends well with other floral scents as well as citrus, herbaceous, woody, and spicy scents.

- Cypress *(Cupressus sempervirens)*

    Cypress is a middle to base note. Cypress oil sits in two elemental camps. Cypress, being a woody scent, is part of the earth element group; however, it also has an affinity with the water element. Although they grow well in any soil, cypress trees love to grow in or around water. You will often find cypress trees near the ocean or in swamps. Cypress has a lovely woody yet airy scent that reminds me of an ocean breeze. Cypress is very earthy and calming and is part of the woody scent group. Cypress blends well with other woody oils as well as spicy, herbaceous, and floral scents.

- Rose Geranium *(Pelargonium graveolens, syn. P. roseum)*

  Rose geranium is a middle note that is steam-distilled from the leaves, twigs, and flowering tops of the plant. Rose geranium is part of the Geraniaceae family. This oil is sweet and powerful. I recommend using only a few drops in a blend as it will take over the whole effect. Rose geranium is also very loving and protective. This oil is sweet in scent yet has a somewhat green quality about it. Rose geranium is part of the floral scent group and blends well with other floral scents as well as with woody, citrus, and resinous oils.

- Myrrh *(Commiphora myrrha)*

  Myrrh is a base note for blending. Myrrh is steam-distilled from the plant's resin and is a member of the Burseraceae family. Myrrh is considered very sacred, and its story has been told throughout time. Myrrh has a slightly spicy, deep, rich scent that is very soothing. Myrrh belongs to the resinous scent group and blends well with other resinous oils as well as with spicy and floral scents.

||||||||||||

For other water element oils, see the appendix.

Suit of Wands
FIRE ELEMENT

The suit of wands within the tarot represents the fire element. All of the cards within the minor arcana of the suit of wands, the royal court, and some major arcana cards relate to the fire element.

Fire is all about passion, desire, transformation, magic, the spark, courage, drama, charisma, change, and creativity. Fire is a masculine energy and is hot and dry. Fire consumes moisture to make the area around it dry, and the heat represents masculine energy that is expansive and reaches outside of one's personal being. Fire does not like to be contained; it prefers to consume. You will find drama and ego in the suit of wands, along with the ability to create and lead with a flare that calls in the masses. This suit is about expansion and outward movement. Many of the essential oils relating to fire come from seeds, citrus oils, and some leaves, twigs, and roots.

An example of a root oil with fire element energy is ginger. Although ginger is a root, it has a spicy, hot taste that calls in the energy of fire. The fire element in our body is represented by the electrical impulses in our body and the heart. Fire's season is summer, its time is noon, and its direction is south. Animals that support fire include fire ant, lion, hyena, tarantula, gecko, gazelle, cheetah, cobra, wild horse, tiger, bee, dragonfly, and snake.

Characteristics of a Fire Individual

- dramatic
- charismatic
- leader
- delegator
- creative

- spark
- willful
- hot-headed
- impulsive
- passionate
- egotistical
- energetic
- angry

Fire Personality Careers

- actors
- CEOs
- politicians
- artists
- salespeople
- leaders

Fire Astrological Signs

- Aries
- Leo
- Sagittarius

Fire Cards

- Queen of Wands
- The Emperor

  The Emperor is the father figure and the companion to the Empress. The Emperor will help set boundaries and get things in order. His is a very structured energy that will help you build your kingdom. He asks you to get things done and requests that they are done correctly. He has power, security, and structure. The Emperor energy will help set up success. At times this card can ask that you seek guidance from an authority figure. This is pure creative power within the confines of structure.

- Strength

Strength is the courage to do what needs to be done with compassion in your heart. This is a time to be grounded, no matter what is going on around you. It may be a difficult time in which you have to make decisions through your internal knowing. Trust yourself. My keywords for this card include courage, trust, strength, unconditional love, and compassion for self and others. This may be a time in which you must own all of who you are. Befriend the beast within instead of trying to tame it. Stand tall, strong, and trust in your wisdom and decisions. In this you will know your strength.

- The Wheel of Fortune

The Wheel of Fortune is a time of change. What goes up must come down, and what has fallen will rise again. As the wheel turns and changes, so do our lives. During this time one may change jobs or change homes; there are many more possibilities. When working with the wheel energy, I like to reduce the 10 down to 1 and call in the energies of the Magician to help manifest the changes that I personally would like to see in my life. All in all, generally this is a positive time with the ability to reap the rewards for the seeds one has sown. Here we find the ending of one cycle and the beginning of a new one.

- Temperance

Despite its alchemical nature, Temperance is a fire element energy that blends two opposites to create something totally new. I often think of this card as fire and water, and what gets created from it as the alchemical blend. This is a card of internal healing, of melding the internal to find balance within. This is a magical time of fluency flowing within as well as without. Pay attention to synchronicities as they may be very important. This could be a very powerful time right now for one's creativity to take form. All in all, this is a time of harmony, healing, and a sense of well-being.

- The Tower

    The Tower is a powerful card with a lot of fire energy. This is a card of chaos and destruction. Things are falling away. These energies were ready to be released. Often this card is about a structure falling; sometimes it represents one's ego. Once the no-longer-needed energies have fallen, new growth begins. Often there is lightning in this card's image; when lightning strikes the earth, it fertilizes it for miles around, allowing for new growth to begin. Sometimes this card can represent a sudden aha moment where everything is suddenly clear and one is awakened, allowing for new direction. Sometimes this is a painful card; at other times it is just clarity.

- The Sun

    The Sun is a bright and powerful energy radiating joy, happiness, and freedom. Often there is a naked boy riding a horse on this card. The boy and the horse represent freedom with nothing left to hide. Be your authentic self. Dance, sing, and enjoy life, for you are now free to be who you want to be. Celebrate and be thankful for life. The Sun is also a card of success.

- Judgment

    The Judgment card is about rebirth and hearing the call. We step into our internal self, our internal cave, and we step out reborn and with a new beginning. Often on this card you will find Archangel Gabriel blowing his horn. This is hearing the call—the call to your true profession, the call to your true self. As with the Death card being water, we can think of Judgment in the same way: going back into the womb of our mother to rest within the cave of water and be reborn. We also can think of fire and how it consumes and transforms. We see wood burn and turn to ash. We can see ourselves transform and shed our skin as with the power of the snake and the power of fire. This card speaks of new beginnings in our true self.

Fire Essential Oils

- Oakwood Absolute *(Quercus robur)*
  Oakwood Absolute is a base note that is solvent-extracted from the wood and bark of the oak tree. Oakwood is a part of the beech family and has a very deep, dark scent with a powerful woody tone. Oakwood is an earth oil as well as a fire oil. Since the oil comes from the wood of the tree, we can find it also has earth energy. Oakwood gets its fire from the tree's connection to lightning and the acorn. This tree seems to attract lightning as it grows taller than other trees and has a higher moisture concentration. Also we have the powerful image of the acorn, the little seed that creates the mighty oak. This oil also is related to the energy of Mars, which is a very fiery planet. The oak is a symbol of power and protection. Woody, sweet, and dark, the scent of oakwood can transport one into the deep forest. Oakwood absolute is in the woody scent group and blends well with other woody scents as well as floral, spicy, and herbaceous scents. I often blend citrus with woody oils.

- Ginger *(Zingiber officinale)*
  Ginger is a middle note. Although ginger is steam-distilled from the roots of the plant, it is a very hot and spicy food. In

this manner you may find ginger in both earth and fire categories. When you eat ginger, it heats up your body. Ginger is a
good source of strength due to the fact that it comes from the
root, which is grounding in spite of its hot, spicy energy. Ginger is part of the Zingiberaceae family and brings grounding,
protection, and security. It also helps aid with passion, creativity, and strength. Ginger has a very powerful, strong scent that
is spicy, hot, and deep. Ginger is part of the spicy scent group
and blends well with other spicy scents as well as with woody,
resinous, and citrus scents.

- Black Pepper *(Piper nigrum)*

  Black pepper is a middle to base note that is steam-distilled
  from the unripe peppercorns of the plant and is part of the
  Piperaceae family. This is a spicy, lightly scented oil—no need
  to worry about sneezing with the oil, unlike the ground pepper! I often use black pepper in my fire blends because of its
  spicy yet uplifting scent. It blends really well with other oils.
  Black pepper is part of the spicy scent group and also blends
  well as with woody, floral, and herbaceous oils. I often blend
  black pepper with citrus.

- Juniper *(Juniperus communis)*

  Juniper is a middle note that is steam-distilled from the
  unripe juniper berries and is part of the Cupressaceae family.
  I think of juniper as a fire and an earth element oil just like its
  family member cedarwood. Juniper is often used for purification and banishing, where it calls in the power of fire. Juniper
  has a woody, earthy scent that calls in the energy of earth. Juniper is a member of the woody scent group and blends well with
  other woody oils as well as with floral, spicy, and herbaceous
  scents.

- Coriander Seed *(Coriandrum sativum)*

  Coriander is a middle note for blending. Coriander is one of my favorite scents. I often diffuse coriander in my home for its powers of protection, its support of change, and its magical scent. Coriander is steam-distilled from the seeds of the plant and is a member of the Apiaceae family. Coriander has a slight spiciness with a light buttery and mildly sweet scent. Coriander is a member of the spicy scent group and blends well with other spicy scents as well as with woody, resinous, and citrus scents.

- Sweet Orange Oil *(Citrus sinensis syn. C. Dulcis)*

  Sweet orange oil is a top note. It is extracted via cold press from the rind of the fruit. Orange oil is a member of the Rutaceae family. I think of all citrus oils as fire oils, but some can fit into other elemental categories, such as lemon, which is also water. Orange oil is just complete joy. Uplifting and gentle, this oil will lift one's heart. Orange has a sweet, light, and citrus scent. Orange oil belongs to the citrus scent group and blends well with other citrus oils as well as with floral, herbaceous, and spicy scents.

|||||||||||

For other fire element oils, see the appendix.

Suit of Swords
AIR ELEMENT

The suit of swords within the tarot relates to the air element. All of the cards within the minor arcana of the suit of swords, the royal court of this suit, and some major arcana cards belong to the air element. The air element is mainly about what is going on in our mind. It is about our thoughts, our fears, anxiety, inspiration, clarity, communication, and truth. We do find more difficult cards to move through due to our fears and anxieties that arise in the suit of swords. This suit is really about clarity and seeing things in a clear and precise manner in order to move through life with truth and courage. The sword cuts through the muck to make things clear. This is a very linear energy that is about getting things down correctly, remembering to dot all the i's and cross all the t's. Speak your truth and be clear about it. This is the least emotional suit in the deck.

The element of air and the suit of swords are hot and wet. Hot represents masculine, expansive energy and the wet speaks to how we receive rain from the atmosphere and how water is evaporated into the air, making this energy wet. Essential oils that are generally air related are derived from the plant's leaves and twigs, which allow for the plant to reach out for more space, growth, and what is needed to create. Air relates to our lungs, our throat, and our mind—all that allows one to breathe, communicate, and think. Air's season is spring, its time is dawn, and its direction is east. Power animals that relate to air include all birds of flight.

Characteristics of an Air Individual

- rational
- studious
- witty
- truthful
- airhead
- spacey
- unreliable
- sharp-tongued
- argumentative
- debater
- communicator

Air Personality Careers

- doctor
- lawyer
- writer
- speaker
- scientist
- scholar
- educator

Air Astrological Signs

- Gemini
- Libra
- Aquarius

Air Cards

- Queen of Swords
- The Fool

  The Fool is the beginning of the journey. The Fool is about taking a leap of faith and jumping off the cliff into the unknown. This energy is a clear-cut energy in that we have chosen to take this leap of faith. We are willing to dive in and experience a new situation. The Fool represents every time we step into something new with personal clarity even though we do not know what the path will entail. The Fool moves ahead with personal confidence and courage. It is a new journey.

- The Lovers

  The Lovers card is not always about a love relationship, but it can be. This card also holds the energy of two paths. One is standing at a crossroads; a decision must be made. This card is about choice. The Lovers can represent a new relationship or a new commitment to that relationship, or it can represent a decision to be made that possibly will lead you into a new direction. This energy also is about letting go of relationships and calling in new ones.

- Justice

  The Justice card is about finding balance in your life and making sure everything is in order. Legal and business issues can appear with this card. This is a card of weighing the scales of Justice, making sure that all is balanced and fair.

- The Star

  The Star is a card of well-being. With the energy of the Star, one feels at peace within, all is well, and one's energy is bright and light. This is not about the external but is more about the internal. What you feel on the inside soon radiates, thereby making your energy bright. Soon all will see the Star within as it shines outward.

Air Essential Oils

- Peppermint *(Mentha x piperita)*

  Peppermint is a top note for blending that is distilled from the leaves of the plant and is part of the Lamiaceae family. I recommend any of the mint oils for your air workings. Peppermint can clear the sinuses and open up the mind; it is stimulating, uplifting, and refreshing. It cools. However, it will burn if you get it in your eyes. Light and airy, peppermint lifts one up. Its scent is sweet and minty, and it belongs to the herbaceous scent group. Peppermint blends well with other herbaceous scents as well as citrus and woody scents.

- Lavender *(Lavandula angustifolia)*

  Lavender is a middle note for blending that is distilled from the leaves and flowering tops of the plant. Lavender is part of the Lamiaceae family. I love lavender. It is light and airy and sweet and flowery at the same time. It has uses in both attraction magic and medicinal purposes. Lavender has been worn and used for many centuries. Since lavender is partially distilled from the leaves, we have the energy of air. Lavender is part of the floral scent group and blends well with other floral scents as well as woody, resinous, and citrus oils.

- Rosemary *(Salvia rosmarinus)*

Rosemary is a middle to top note for blending that is often listed as a fire and air oil, so use it either way in a blend. I use rosemary more often in my air blends. Rosemary is steam-distilled from the leaves and flowering tops of the plant, and it is part of the Lamiaceae family. Rosemary is often used to help with memory. When I was studying for my aromatherapy boards, I made a blend of rosemary and grapefruit to help with increasing my retention of the material. Rosemary is a lovely scent that is herbaceous, medicinal, minty, and uplifting. Rosemary is part of the herbaceous scent group and blends well with other herbaceous oils as well as woody and citrus oils.

- Violet Absolute *(Viola odorata)*

Violet is a base to middle note for blending that is extracted via solvent extraction of the plant's leaves and flowers. It is a member of the Violaceae family. Violet absolute has a very different scent. Rather than smelling floral, it smells green. It is grassy, deep, and earthy. Violet absolute is often used in the perfume industry but not often in the aromatherapy industry. I personally love this scent. For our purposes, violet absolute will be under the floral scent group; it blends well with other floral scents as well as woody, resinous, and citrus oils.

For other air element oils, see the appendix.

Part Two

Pulling It
All Together

An Introduction to Essential Oils

What are essential oils, where do they come from, and how can they help us shift our personal energies? These are questions we will answer in this chapter. Essential oils often play a part in the survival of the plant in some form. The functions of the essential oils may be different for each plant based on where the oil is derived from on the plant. Not all plants produce essential oils.

Aromatherapy is the use of essential oils to encourage health, balance, and well-being. Although aromatherapy is often used for physical health, essential oils can also be used spiritually, assisting spiritual and mental development. Aromatherapy is extremely powerful for assistance with the mind and emotions and is often used to help with depression and anxiety. Aromatherapy can call in joy, peace, euphoria, or relaxation, depending on the scent, chemical constituents, and the actions of the essential oil used. Some essential oils are considered stimulating, and some are relaxing. Let's take a look at where essential oils come from and how they assist their plant as well as how they can assist us.

Essential oils are derived from many different plant parts. Oils are extracted from bark, flowers, fruit, grasses, leaves, needles, twigs, resins, roots, and wood. Generally, each essential oil comes from one plant part. In this book we will be discussing the spiritual aspects of the essential oils rather than the clinical. The key questions here are what plant anatomy did the oil come from? How does that essential oil work with its plant parent, and how can this essential oil work with us? What elemental category does this essential oil belong to?

I first learned of this concept of plant part/plant energy from one of my favorite aromatherapy teachers, Jade Shutes. Shutes is the creator and owner of the School of Aromatic Studies as well as the president of NAHA, the National Association for Holistic Aromatherapy. I read several articles by Shutes discussing plant morphology, or the study of plants' form and structure. We will use this system to help determine how an essential oil can assist us spiritually via where it is derived from on the plant. Shutes speaks of morphology as a way of intuitively working with essential oils based upon the correspondences and energetics within each individual plant's form and its job or role within the plant.

We also need to remember that plants are living beings sharing their individual magic with us for our healing and personal development. Essential oils are to be respected and their spirit energies embraced as gifts from our Mother Gaia. Let's take a look at the different plant parts that essential oils are derived from and how they work with us as humans.

|||||||||||||

Essential oils are highly concentrated plant materials and plant energies that can be considered dangerous if not used correctly. Always dilute essential oils with a carrier oil. Never ingest essential oils unless directed by a physician, and always check precautions on every oil that you intend to use on your body or in your environment. Keep essential oils away from children and pets. If creating an essential oil body spray, it is best to not spray in the face due to the chemical constituents of some essential oils such as peppermint or cinnamon, which can burn the eyes and mucous membranes. You will find precautions on all essential oils listed in this book in the appendix.

Roots, Wood, and Bark

Roots

The roots help to ground the plant, connecting it to Mother Earth and therefore stabilizing it. The roots also nourish the plant and supply the necessary nutrients, hormones, and water absorption for the plant to survive and develop. The roots bring in powerful grounding energy for the plant as well as for us as humans. We can choose to work with root oils to ground, center, and call in stability and healthy, nurturing energy. The roots relate to the root chakra as they help us find our security and stability as well as supply a foundation for survival.

ROOT OILS: Angelica root, ginger, galangal, Australian sandalwood, turmeric, valerian, vetiver

Wood

The wood of a plant or tree calls in the energies of protection, stability, and balance. Think of how the wood of the tree is supportive as its outer foundation, the trunk. The wood allows the tree to grow to its desired height, maintain a balanced state in times of storms or high winds, and also to act as protection against insects, birds, and any other form of possible invasion. The wood also helps conduct nutrients and water up to the leaves, stems, and flowers. The wood asks one to go within and seek internal wisdom. It supports balance and strength as well as protection. Again, this is grounding, nurturing, and balancing root chakra energy.

Bark

The bark of a plant or tree is very similar to wood as it is also a protectant against invasion of any kind. As you can see, roots, wood, and bark are all very grounding, protective, stabilizing, and nurturing energy. Think root chakra, the suit of pentacles, earthy and grounding energy, earth element energy.

> WOOD AND BARK OILS: Agarwood, amyris, Virginia cedarwood, cinnamon bark, ho wood, oakwood absolute, palo santo, Australian sandalwood

Resins

Resin drips out of the bark of the plant or tree as a form of healing for the plant. This can help with insect attacks, disease, or general wear and tear. The resin feels like a very gentle, healing, and spiritual energy. Resins can come in the form of pitch, gums, oleoresins, and fossil resins. Sandra Kynes states in her book *Mixing Essential Oils for Magic* that she believes resins are the lifeblood of the plant, therefore calling in the energy of vitality. So, in working with resins in an essential oil blend or by single oil, we are calling in the energy of healing as well as vitality, life energy, and spirituality. I relate resins to the water element and its healing, spiritual, flowing energy.

> RESINS: Benzoin, fir (balsam), frankincense, galbanum, myrrh, opopanax

Leaves, Needles, Twigs, and Flowering Tops

I like to think of leaves and twigs as giving us the ability to reach out for what we want in life. Leaves burst forth in springtime signaling new growth and vitality. Twigs call in the energy of wood, adding grounding and stability to the growth of new life. The leaves are the new energy and growth for the plant and reach out and above for sun and air. There is a sense of freedom in the energy of a leaf. Some essential oils come from only the leaf and some from leaves and twigs in combination. I consider many of the leaf and leaf-twig oils as belonging to the air element.

LEAVES: Allspice, bay laurel, bergamot mint, cinnamon leaf, citronella, clove, eucalyptus, rose geranium, lemon myrtle, myrtle, niaouli, patchouli, petitgrain, tea tree, violet absolute

Needles, just like leaves, call in vitality and freedom and help one to expand, breathe, and reach out. Like leaves, new needles arrive each spring and bring in new life to the tree. Many of the fir, pine, and spruce essential oils are derived from a combination of needles and twigs. Needles often fit into the elements of earth, air, and fire. Earth because they come from the tree and have an earthy quality and scent to them. Air because they call in a sense of freedom and expansion and help with the breath, and fire because they bring in vitality, like a spark. Needles purify and have magical properties that relate to the fire element. Also think of dry needles and how they burn quickly!

NEEDLES: Cypress, balsam fir, scotch pine, pinon pine, black spruce

Twigs always work in conjunction with leaves. You will never find an essential oil derived just from twigs. Twigs enhance the leaf oils with the qualities of wood and bark. Twigs call in strength as they create the foundation for the leaves to grow upon and help the leaves reach out and upward. Often the combination of leaves and twigs will fit into the air element, but with the addition of the twig, you will find earth, air, and fire elements in this category.

TWIGS AND LEAVES: cypress, petitgrain, tea tree

There are also twig and needle combinations. The twig calls in the wood and bark energy to enhance the energy of the needle. Twigs bring in strength, protection, and grounding support to the needle.

TWIGS AND NEEDLES: cypress, Douglas fir, pine, spruce

In the combination of leaves with flowering tops, we find the qualities and magical energies of both the leaf and the flower. The energy of the flower can shift the elemental energy of the oil and call in the water element (as in the essential oils of clary sage and lemon balm), air element qualities (as in peppermint and lavender), as well as some fire energies (as in basil and hyssop, whose leaves are spicy in nature). We also find the earth element with Spanish sage. Although many of these essential oils fit into the air element category, you can see how they can fit into more than one elemental energy.

LEAVES AND FLOWERING TOPS: Basil, catnip, clary sage, hyssop, lavender, lemon balm, marjoram, oregano, peppermint, rosemary, Spanish sage, spearmint, thyme, yarrow

Flowers

The flowers work hard for the plants—think of how bees are attracted to flowers for pollination. In this manner, the flowers attract as well as help produce the sexuality of the plant, calling in the energy of reproduction. Humans have worn perfume for years to attract a mate. This is what the flower essential oils can do for us. With flower oils we can attract what we desire for our use and benefit. I think of the energy of flowers as belonging to the water element. The associated chakra energy of flowers is the heart chakra.

FLOWERS: German chamomile, Roman chamomile, helichrysum, jasmine, lavender, neroli, rose, ylang-ylang

Fruit

In working with the energy of fruit oils, you can think of the word *fruition*. The fruit of the plant is the end product. The fruit is what the plant has been working toward—its destination, so to speak. We can work with fruit oils in the same manner. When adding a fruit oil to a blend or just working with a single fruit essential oil, you are calling in the end result, the masterpiece, embracing success and the final outcome. Fruit essential oils have quite a bit of sun energy, so these oils can also call in the energies associated with the sun: joy, happiness, and celebration. Most fruit essential oils relate to the fire element as they represent our success, our glory, our individuality, or complete manifestation in reality. Some fruit essential oils will relate to the water element because of their cleansing qualities as well as their juicy energy.

FRUITS: Bergamot, grapefruit, juniper, lemon, lime, mandarin, orange, black pepper, tangerine

Seeds

Seed oils represent pure potential, new beginnings, and change. Seeds are often carried on the wings of the winds to a new home in the earth where they begin their new growth. In any new adventures in life, it is wise to start a blend with a seed oil as the seed of potential and growth for your endeavor. Seeds generally represent fire element because they represent the spark that starts the flame.

SEEDS: Anise, angelica seed, cardamom, carrot, coriander, cumin, dill, fennel, nutmeg, parsley

■ ■ ■ ■

As you can see, there is a magical system here for blending oils, working with the elements of essential oils, and communicating through your blend what your intentions are for your personal development. Although we have categorized oils based on where they are derived from in the plant, note that sometimes essential oils can fit into more than one category. Although ginger is a root oil (earth element), it is also spicy in taste, creating a fire energy and fire element oil. You can use ginger in either manner. You can also look at the essential oil of cinnamon, which comes from the bark and sometimes the leaves of the plant. Although this oil may be categorized as earthy when derived from the bark, I actually think of it as fire due to its spicy scent.

When you have an essential oil that fits into more than one category, use your personal preference to determine why you are using that essential oil in your blend or which category that essential oil falls into for you.

6

Blending
Essential Oils

Working with essential oils through the system of morphology is just one way to create a blend. In this chapter we will learn to blend essential oils in three different manners: by note, scent group, and elemental energy, as well as morphology.

Blending by Note

When I first started aromatherapy school, we learned to blend by note. This is the system that is most used by clinical aromatherapists as well as perfumers. Blending by note is a simple system where we are creating a chord, a blending of three different essential oils that creates a whole. In a blend there can be more than one chord. Let's start with a discussion on how a chord is built in an essential oil blend.

Choosing the Notes in Your Chord

A chord in music is built on three notes: the root, the third, and the fifth of a chosen scale. In aromatherapy a chord is built on three types of essential oils: a base note (meaning a deep, earthy note), a middle note (a melding or heart note), and a top note, or head note. These three notes create the chord of scent. Below we will discuss the three different types of notes and how they work together in your blend.

Base Note

A base note is the grounding or fixative note in a blend that sets the blend's foundation and holds down its energy. Base notes offer up the scent that will last the longest. This grounding note helps to slow down the evaporation rate of the top note. Base note scents can last several days; if applied to the body, they can stay within the body for up to 72 hours. Base notes are generally earthy, grounding scents. These are scents generally derived from the roots, wood, bark, or resins of a plant.

Examples of essential oils that are base notes are amyris, benzoin, patchouli, frankincense, myrrh, Virginia cedarwood, cocoa absolute, oakmoss, oakwood absolute, Australian sandalwood, vanilla absolute, and vetiver.

When blending, decide what size bottle you are using and then start the blend with your base note. A half-ounce bottle would be a 15-milliliter bottle. In this size bottle, you would only need 1 drop of the base note to get started. I recommend starting small and testing your blend before creating a larger portion. See below for the bottle size and drop proportion for base notes.

½-ounce bottle = 15ml = 1 drop of the base note

1-ounce bottle = 30ml = 3 drops base note

2-ounce bottle = 60ml = 6 drops of base note

4-ounce bottle = 120ml = 12 drops of base note

Middle Note

The middle note, or heart note, helps weave the blend together. This note releases its scent a few minutes after application. As my aromatherapy teacher Shanti Dechen states in her workbook *Aroma-*

therapy Certification Level 1 Course, the middle note can last from 4–6 hours and will generally work on the emotional level. Middle notes are generally derived from leaves, twigs, needles, and flowers.

Examples of essential oils that would fall into the middle note category are black pepper, catnip, Roman chamomile, German chamomile, cypress, fir, rose geranium, juniper, lavender, lemon balm, marjoram, pine, rosemary, spearmint, and violet.

When adding in the middle note, use the chart below:

½-ounce bottle = 15ml = 2 drops middle note

1-ounce bottle = 30ml = 4 drops middle note

2-ounce bottle = 60ml = 8 drops middle note

4-ounce bottle = 120ml = 16 drops middle note

Top Note

The top note is the first scent you will encounter when smelling a blend. This top note will evaporate in the blend the fastest and last 2–4 hours in the body. The top note tends to work with the spirit. These oils are generally derived from the fruits, flowers, and sometimes spicy scented oils. Some top note oils would be lemon, orange, lime, peppermint, and anise.

When adding the top note, use the chart below:

½-ounce bottle = 15ml = 3 drops top note

1-ounce bottle = 30ml = 5 drops top note

2-ounce bottle = 60ml = 10 drops top note

4-ounce bottle = 120ml = 20 drops top note

■ ■ ■ ■

Although we have categorized these essential oils as base, middle, or top note oils, essential oils are very complex and can fit into more than one category. Some middle notes can blend in as top notes, and some base notes can blend in as middle notes.

TOP NOTES: Anise, basil, bergamot, cardamom, cinnamon, clary sage, eucalyptus, grapefruit, hyssop, lemon, lemongrass, lime, myrtle, neroli, sweet orange, palmarosa, peppermint, petitgrain, rose, Spanish sage, spearmint, tea tree, tangerine, thyme

TOP TO MIDDLE NOTES: Angelica seed, basil, bergamot, bay laurel, clary sage, eucalyptus, fennel, lemongrass, pine, tea tree, thyme

MIDDLE NOTES: Bay laurel, black pepper, cardamom, Roman chamomile, cypress, eucalyptus, fennel, balsam fir, rose geranium, ginger, helichrysum, ho wood, hyssop, juniper, lavender, lemon balm, marjoram, neroli, nutmeg, oregano, pine, rosemary, Spanish sage, yarrow

MIDDLE TO BASE NOTES: Angelica root, benzoin, black pepper, Virginia cedarwood, clary sage, cypress, German chamomile, jasmine, ylang-ylang

BASE NOTES: Amyris, benzoin, cocoa absolute, frankincense, ginger, jasmine, myrrh, oakmoss, oakwood absolute, patchouli, Australian sandalwood, turmeric, valerian, vanilla absolute, vetiver, ylang-ylang

Starting with a ½ ounce bottle, add three drops of your top note, two drops of your middle note, and one drop of your base note; simple as 3-2-1! The problem is that if you just choose from the top, middle, and base note oils, they may not blend well together in the scent category. You should always start with three oils, let the blend sit for a couple of hours, and then smell and see how they are blending.

Blending by Scent Group

By blending with scent groups of essential oils, you will find oils that will blend well together. You can use the blending by note process to create the blend and then choose oils from the scent and elemental groupings. If you remember the information on morphology and how essential oils were divided up based on where they were derived from on the plant, this scent grouping will feel very similar. Let's take a look at the different groupings: woody, spicy, floral, citrus, herbaceous, and resinous. Scent groups are used to create blends in the aromatherapy world as well as the world of perfumery. These scent groupings have been used for many moons.

Woody

Woody scents are those earthy, deep, rooted oils. These oils are often but not always also base note oils.

Woody oils are oils such as amyris, Virginia cedarwood, cypress, balsam fir, juniper, oakmoss, oakwood absolute, patchouli, pine, Australian sandalwood, spruce, valerian, and vetiver.

- Woody oils blend well with all other scent groups.

Spicy

Spicy scents are just what they sound like: these oils generally have a kick to them of some type, whether it be in the scent or the taste of the plant. These oils will bring some life into a blend.

Spicy oils can be oils such as anise, bay laurel, benzoin, black pepper, cinnamon, clove, coriander, fennel, ginger, myrtle, nutmeg, petitgrain, tarragon, and thyme.

- Spicy oils blend well with woody, citrus, resinous, and floral essential oils.

Sometimes spicy oils can have a sensitizing or irritating effect on the skin. Always remember to do a patch test on your skin prior to applying to the body. Dilute your oil with a carrier oil and then apply 1 to 2 drops to the inner forearm. Don't get this area wet. Watch for any skin irritation or sensitivities to this area. Wait 48 hours and if there is no reaction, then you are ready to use. If at any time you notice a reaction, apply just the carrier oil, not water, to that area to help dilute the power of the essential oil.

Floral

Floral scents are sweet and flowery scents. These oils are often derived from flowers and some leaves and flowering tops. Floral oils are often top to middle note oils. Floral oils call in sweetness to the blend.

Floral oils are oils such as Roman chamomile, rose geranium, jasmine, lavender, neroli, palmarosa, rose, vanilla, ylang-ylang, and violet absolute. Although violet is a flower, it sometimes can fit into the green scent grouping because of its green scent. Violet does not have a flowery scent as it is derived from the flower and green leaves of the plant.

- Floral oils blend well with woody, citrus, spicy, and resinous essential oils.

Citrus

Citrus oils are derived from the fruits of the plant. These oils call in joy, brightness, and vitality to a blend. These oils are often top to middle notes.

Citrus oils are oils such as bergamot, grapefruit, lemon, lemon balm, lemongrass, lime, orange, and tangerine.

- Citrus oils blend well with woody, spicy, floral, and herbaceous essential oils.

Green

There is a green scent group used most often in perfumery. There are not many scents in this category. Essential oils that can fit into the green scent are clary sage, galbanum, lavender absolute, lovage, petitgrain, and violet absolute. The green scent embraces the smell of freshly cut grass, dewy leaves, and the scent of spring in the air. Reference *Essence and Alchemy: A Natural History of Perfume* by Mandy Aftel.

- Green oils blend well with floral, woody, and citrus essential oils.

Herbaceous

Herbaceous oils are often derived from the leaves, twigs, and sometimes flowering tops of a plant. These oils carry a bright, uplifting energy. These notes are often middle to top note oils.

Herbaceous oils are oils such as basil, catnip, citronella, clary sage, eucalyptus, helichrysum, hyssop, lavender, marjoram, oregano, peppermint, rosemary, Spanish sage, spearmint, tea tree, and thyme.

- Herbaceous oils blend well with woody and citrus oils.

Resinous

Resinous oils are generally thicker oils because they are derived from the sap, gums, and resins of a plant. These oils are generally middle to base note oils.

Resinous oils are oils such as benzoin, frankincense, galbanum, myrrh, and opopanax.

- Resinous oils blend well with floral, spicy, and woody oils.

■ ■ ■ ■

Blending by scent group allows you to choose essential oils that will work well together in a blend. Blending by note will help to create a solid and powerful blend.

Blending by Elemental Energy

When I first started blending essential oils, I blended by elemental energy. I was mainly creating blends that were related to tarot and the chakras. This made blending easy and powerful. Blending by element embraces the energy of the tarot card you are working with. Let's take a look.

Earth Element

The suit of pentacles is earth element, along with several of the major arcana cards, so working with woods, bark, roots, and resins would be my first go-to. You can just blend together oils such as vetiver, Australian sandalwood, frankincense, oakwood absolute, and patchouli. This will give you a solid grounding blend.

You can also choose to add another elemental energy to the blend if you would like. Maybe you are starting a new business and are working with the Empress as your guide. You are working to call in abundance, growth, and a solid foundation, as well as creative energy and beauty to your work space. Then maybe you would add a fire oil for the creative spark and a flower oil for the energy of beauty and attraction. If you look at the scent groups, you will see that generally woods blend well with fruits and flowers. You can choose from those scent groups to create your blend.

Water Element

When working with the water element and the suit of cups, or any of the major arcana cards that relate to the water element, you could work with oils that support one's emotions, intuition, and heart energies. You will need to discover which of the qualities you are wishing to embrace and connect those qualities to their elemental energies.

Water element oils are generally resins and floral scent groups. Do you want to create a flow, open your heart chakra, call in your intuition and psychic abilities, or find a new love relationship? Are you trying to heal your heart?

Let's say you are working with the Death card, which corresponds to the water element. There is a lot of change going on in your life right now, and you just want to be able to let go and move forward to a new beginning. The Death card energy can be difficult at times when things fall away unexpectedly. I would start with a resin. Remember that resins heal the plant they are a part of, so a resin will also help heal your emotional energies. Using an oil such as benzoin (a resin) as your base note would be lovely. Then you can add in a floral oil for loving support and attraction to new beginnings. Lastly, you can choose to work with cypress, the oil of the Death card. Cypress is woody, yet cypress is attracted to water. (See chapter 2 for essential oil–tarot correspondences.)

Now your blend consists of a base note of benzoin, a middle note of cypress, and a top note of rose (floral). Your blend contains two water oils and a wood oil.

Fire Element

Fire oils and the suit of wands, along with any major arcana cards that relate to the fire element, call in charisma, courage, strength, magic, the spark, transformation, change, passion, and desire. Fire elemental oils come mainly from the spicy and citrus scent groups. Fire elemental oils can be made from seeds, leaves, leaves and twigs, and fruit as well as bark. Let's say you are working with the Queen of Wands to start your speaking career. The Queen of Wands will create the perfect cauldron of magic for you. Using a seed oil to start with would be great as seed oils are the spark, the potential for growth.

Blending together anise, a fire and seed oil, along with other fire oils such as orange, lime, cinnamon, clove, petitgrain, and black pepper, and then adding some Virginia cedarwood as a base note, would be a lovely Queen of Wands blend.

Air Element

Air oils relate to the suit of swords and the major arcana cards that relate to the air element. Air essential oils call in the energy of inspiration, hope, clarity, communication, freedom, and balance. Maybe you have an exam to take and you are working with the Queen of Swords to help you keep a good study schedule as well as help you comprehend and memorize the needed material.

Working with oils such as peppermint, eucalyptus, rosemary, and lemongrass would be lovely for an air blend. Generally air elemental oils will come from the leaves and twigs of a plant.

■ ■ ■ ■

With this approach to blending, you can just add together only air oils or only fire oils, for example. You don't have to create a blend using base, middle, and top note; just blend with the element in mind. If you decide to add another element for a boost to your blend, then use the note system to help merge the blend together. When not using the note system in some manner, you may have a blend in which the scent can evaporate quickly.

Blending by Morphology

We have already discussed morphology in some detail, and now we will learn how to blend using the plant anatomies. Your intention for the blend is the key to creating a powerful and magical blend. Knowing why you wish to create the blend is the first step. Here is an example.

When I created my Magician blend, I wanted a blend that would give me the power to manifest my desires into reality. I wanted to totally embrace the energy of the Magician. I thought about what energies I wanted to call in prior to blending. Here is what I chose for the blend, and it turned out beautifully.

The Magician Blend

- A seed oil for the potential to become: Anise
- A root oil for nourishment, structure, and grounding: Vetiver
- Leaves and twigs to reach out for what I want and need: Petitgrain
- A flower for attraction: Ylang-ylang
- A fruit for fruition: Lemon
- An oil for all four elements since the Magician has all four elements on his table:

    Earth element: Virginia cedarwood and vanilla

    Water element: Benzoin and lemon

    Fire element: Black pepper and cinnamon

    Air element: Lavender and Virginia cedarwood

This is one of my favorite blends, and this system really hones in on creating by intention, which is how all blends need to be born.

In working with morphology, here are the considerations to keep in mind:

- What is your intention?
- What plant parts do you wish to use and why?
- What scent groups do these oils belong to? Will they blend well together?

- Do you want to use the note system or not? When creating the Magician blend, I did not use the note system; I just chose which oils I wanted and used my intuition for the number of drops per oil. I did end up with enough oils in the blend to have base, middle, and top notes.

- Always check precautions of the oils you are using in your blend.

- Are you creating an oil-based blend or a water-based blend? When creating a water-based spray, add some jojoba oil to help the oils blend well with the water. The jojoba oil will be the first ingredient into the bottle—add just enough jojoba to cover the bottom of the bottle. If creating an oil-based blend, which carrier oil do you wish to use and why?

- What size bottle do you wish to work with?

■ ■ ■ ■

Once you have all this information available, then you are ready to blend. Remember to let the oil blend sit for two hours and then test the scent. If you want to adjust the scent a bit and add a few more drops of one or two of the essential oils, then you can do so now. Once satisfied, allow the blend to sit for three days and gently swirl daily while thinking about your intention. After three days, you are ready for use. Remember that the scent can adjust a bit more over time.

Carrier Oils

What is a carrier oil and how can you use them to sustain the power of the blend? How can a carrier oil help with the intention behind the blend? These are great questions that can lead to the enhancement of your creation.

A carrier oil is a vegetable, nut, or seed oil that we use to contain and open up the scent of our essential oils. These oils are the base of the blend and are fixed in nature, meaning that they are not subject to rapid change. In a sense, carrier oils help to carry the essential oils into the body. Essential oils do not blend well in water and will need jojoba oil to allow the scent of the essential oils to blend in when creating water-based sprays. Water-based sprays can grow bacteria so they must be used up within two months unless alcohol is added as a preservative.

Carrier oils also add volume to your blend as well as an extra layer of protection to the skin. Skin irritations are more likely to surface when applying oils without a carrier. Essential oils should never be applied to the skin without a carrier oil or diluted in a water-based spray. Carrier oils also help to sustain the length of the scent on your skin by protecting and slowing down the evaporation rate of the essential oils. Carrier oils, like essential oils, should be stored in a dark and cool space. Some carrier oils will do best refrigerated. Working with carrier oils can add to your blend not only in the form of skin protection and evaporation rate and volume, but they also carry their own personal elemental and magical qualities. There are many different carrier oils, but I only tend to use a few when blending for the tarot. Listed below are the carrier oils that I use in my blends and their magical properties.

Sweet Almond Oil *(Prunus amygdalus var. dulcis)*

ELEMENTAL ENERGY: Air and fire

Sweet almond oil is derived from the fruit or nut of the almond tree. I use this oil as the main ingredient for my earth and water blends such as the Queen of Pentacles, the Queen of Cups, the Empress, and the High Priestess, and any earth and water elemental major arcana cards. Although this oil would fit into the fire elemental energy because it is derived from the fruit or nut, it carries energies that relate to the feminine. Sweet almond oil is related to the goddess Venus, therefore calling in the energies of beauty, attraction, fertility, growth, abundance, and wisdom.

Camellia Seed Oil *(Camellia oleifera)*

ELEMENTAL ENERGY: Fire and water

Camellia seed oil is derived from the seeds of the plant, calling in fire elemental energy, yet this oil has a very feminine feel about it. I love this oil and add a bit of it to a feminine blend to enhance beauty, attraction, and fertility. This oil is also quite beautiful on the skin. The leaves are used to produce tea, and these tea leaves can be used for divination purposes, which is the feminine energy of internal knowledge and wisdom. This plant tends to like morning sun and afternoon shade, therefore calling in the feminine through the energy of the shade. You can use this oil in totality for your blend if you like or add in a pinch to a blend for its lovely feminine qualities.

Fractionated Coconut Oil *(Cocos nucifera L.)*

ELEMENTAL ENERGY: Water

Fractionated coconut oil is distilled from regular coconut oil, which is derived from the meat of the fruit. This creates an oil that contains only medium-chain triglycerides, which cause the oil to stay in a liquid form rather than harden with cooler temperatures as pure coconut oil does. Fractionated coconut oil is feminine in nature and calls in the energy of the moon. Very healing and calming, this oil also carries the magical properties of protection and purification due to its water nature. This oil can be used fully as the carrier oil without adding jojoba oil. Fractionated coconut oil has an extremely long shelf life and therefore is really useful for oil-based blends. In traditional aromatherapy, this oil is not considered a complete oil and therefore is sometimes not used by some aromatherapists due to its chemically altered nature.

Evening Primrose Oil *(Oenothera biennis)*

ELEMENTAL ENERGY: Fire and water

Evening primrose oil is derived from the seeds of the plant, therefore calling in the energy of fire, yet this plant's flowers only bloom in the night. Evening primrose embraces the feminine through its night blooming as well as its ability to protect and assist in times of change. I add a couple tablespoons of this oil to a 4-ounce blend of the Moon, the Hanged Man, or any water element blend where the intention is to increase the energy of night vision and protection.

Jojoba Oil *(Simmondsia chinensis)*

ELEMENTAL ENERGY: Fire and water

Jojoba oil is derived from the bean of the plant and is actually a wax. This is very feminine energy. The jojoba plant has both male and female plants. The male plant produces the flowers, and the female plant produces the seeds or beans. Jojoba feels very healing, protective, and balancing to me. Jojoba oil can also help with creating a focused energy on your intention for the blend. This oil can become cloudy because of its waxy quality but will liquefy at room temperature. Because this oil is a wax, it tends to have a longer shelf life than other oils. Due to this fact, I add about 2 tablespoons to a blend of 4 ounces to keep the blend from going rancid quickly. When an oil becomes rancid, it can become toxic and may lose its fresh scent, leaving a less than desirable smell. Keeping your oil blends stored in dark bottles and in a dark, cool space will also help slow down the breakdown of the oils.

Olive Oil *(Olea europaea)*

ELEMENTAL ENERGY: Fire and water

Although I personally do not use olive oil for my blends, I realize that many folks have olive oil on their kitchen shelves and may want to create a blend with what they have available, which is perfectly acceptable. Olive oil is derived from the fruit of the plant. The olive speaks of peace and the promise of a new day. Think of how it is said that when the olive branch is extended, it offers peace and new beginnings. Olive oil also speaks of prosperity and abundance, making it a great oil to add to blends with the intention of financial growth.

Sunflower Oil *(Helianthus annuus)*

ELEMENTAL ENERGY: Fire

Sunflower oil is derived from the seeds of the plant. The sunflower desires the warmth of the sun. It is pure masculine, solar energy. I use this oil for all of my fire and air blends because of its expansive energy. This oil is powerful in seeing and becoming an individual. Sunflower oil can call in joy, happiness, and success, and it works well with supporting loss, sadness, and depression.

■ ■ ■

As you can see, when creating a blend, you can choose a carrier oil or oils based on their elemental energy and their powerful magical properties.

Adding a pinch of jojoba to all blends is very useful in keeping your scent fresh and vital for a longer period of time, maximizing the shelf life of your blends.

Always remember that when creating an essential oil blend, your intention is the key to success. Start with your chosen tarot archetype and then your intention and keywords that support the energy of this archetype. Choose your oils based on whichever system you wish to use to create your beautiful, magical blend.

7

Adding Crystals and Gemstones to Your Cauldron

Rocks came into my life at an early age. I remember my Kindergarten teacher telling us that if we found a rock with a white line that went all around the circumference of the rock, then we have found a magic rock. She told us to hold the rock and make a wish, then toss the rock behind us. If we could find that rock again, then our wish would come true. I did this magic and wished for a playhouse with all the trimmings and dress-up clothing. About three years later, my two older brothers built me a small log cabin playhouse in the backyard. My parents bought me play furniture that included a little mop and broom. My sister started sewing and creating costumes and dresses for play. Everything I had wished for happened; it just took time.

After this experience I would find rocks and wash them and try to polish them up for later magical use. To this day I love rocks. Although all rocks, crystals, and stones come from the earth, not all stones carry only the earth element energy. Each crystal or stone vibrates at their own frequency. Some will have a low frequency (relating to the earth element) and some will have a high frequency (relating to the spiritual realm). You will have many frequencies in between with different levels of vibrations. Stones also have different minerals laced and speckled within them. These minerals help determine the energies of the stone. Let's take a look at calcite. Calcite is rich in calcium carbonate. Some stones will carry more than one elemental energy due to their wide range of frequencies and their chemical compositions.

In *The Book of Stones* by Robert Simmons and Naisha Ahsian, Simmons speaks of how crystals and stones help balance the body and aura through calling in the needed vibration and healing energy that is required to balance the body system as a whole. When coming in contact with a specific stone, that stone's frequency will resonate with your personal frequencies and call in more of the crystal's vibrational energies into your auric field and body. If the stone is vibrating at a high frequency, your frequency will increase; at a low frequency, your personal frequency will lower.

Crystals and stones also help balance the body, allowing the minerals inherent within the crystal to vibrate with your personal corresponding mineral level within your body. So when holding a calcite stone, the calcium minerals within the stone will resonate with the calcium within your body. This in turn makes your body believe that you now have more calcium. Your brain will send this message to the body, which therefore can bring into balance any calcium-related illnesses. Lowering your body frequency will help to ground and center, while raising your frequency can help connect to your intuition and your guides and angels through the crown chakra. In this manner you can work with a stone to create the energies needed to help you move forward on your chosen path.

In the tarot apothecary we will work with stones in two ways. The easiest way to work with a particular stone is to wear it. Work with a stone that you can adorn yourself with in the form of a necklace, bracelet, ring, or earrings. This brings beauty and color into your world and allows you to vibrate at your chosen energy. The second manner in which we will work with stones is to add them directly into your aromatherapy blend. You can purchase very small pieces of stone or chips to add to your blend and help raise or lower its vibration. The stone and your intention will help call in the required energies of your archetype for personal advancement.

Personally, when I move into a new year or a new energy, I often find myself attracted to different stones. In my Lovers year, I was attracted to lapis lazuli. Lapis is a beautiful blue stone that helps work with the throat chakra and relates to the element of air. The Lovers is also an air element energy. Recently I moved into my Chariot year, which is a water element year. Since the shift in energy from air (the Lovers) into water (the Chariot), I am suddenly attracted to rose quartz, which is a member of the water element family. I feel the compassion and love from the rose quartz supporting me on my journey forward.

Clearing Your Stones

Stones and crystals will hold on to the energies that they come in contact with. When you purchase a crystal, remember that this crystal may have been held by many people prior to your purchase. You want this stone to be clear and to release any negative energies it may have picked up along the way. In this manner, once the stone is cleared, it will want to resonate with your personal energies.

There are many ways in which to clear a crystal. It can be as simple as running water over the crystal. This simple method is often done and is trustworthy. Some crystals will not tolerate water, so be careful and research your crystal first before applying this method of clearing. Crystals such as selenite will dissolve due to their salt and mineral content. You can search the "Mohs hardness scale" online for any stones listed under the number five and below. These stones will not do well in water.

Another way in which to clear your stones is to use salt. Just fill a bowl with salt and allow your stones to sit for at least two hours for a clearing. To clear your stones, you can also use smoke or incense or you can place your stones under the full moon. Sunlight also can be used as a clearing method, but again, research your crystal before applying this method as sunlight can leach color from certain stones.

The Elemental Energies of Stones

Since we are working with archetypes and their elemental energies, I have categorized the stones and crystals listed below by their elemental energy. I have chosen stones that are readily available to you and are most commonly used.

Stones of the Earth Element

Earth element stones are often black, brown, and sometimes red or green in color. These stones will vibrate at a lower vibration and help ground, center, and root you into your being. They will help you walk your path with a solidity and belief in yourself.

> agate (moss), amber, Apache tears, aventurine,
> bloodstone, calcite (red), chrysanthemum stone,
> flint, garnet, hematite, jade, jasper, jet, obsidian,
> onyx, peridot, pyrite, ruby, serpentine, shaman's
> stone, smoky quartz, tiger's-eye, tourmaline

Stones of the Water Element

Water element stones are often blue or pink in color and will relate to the second chakra as well as the fourth chakra of the heart. These stones will work with your emotions, compassion, and love energies and create a gentle flow in your life.

aqua aura quartz, aquamarine, aventurine, blue
lace agate, chrysocolla, emerald, kunzite, larimar,
moonstone, opal, rhodochrosite, rose quartz

Stones of the Fire Element

Fire element stones are often red, orange, or yellow in color and
relate to the third chakra, the will to become. These stones will help
call in courage, passion, creativity, energy, confidence, and charisma.
These stones will be the spark.

Apache tears, calcite (orange), calcite (red),
carnelian, cinnabar, citrine, fire agate,
fire opal, malachite, sun stone, topaz

Stones of the Air Element

Air element stones are usually blue, purple, white, or clear in color.
These stones will call in clarity, inspiration, communication skills,
and a sense of freedom.

amethyst, aventurine (blue), azurite, calcite (blue),
celestite, danburite, fluorite, labradorite, lapis lazuli,
moonstone, sapphire (blue), selenite, sodalite

■ ■ ■

Create your blend and drop in some gem chips of your choice to add
more power and magic to your creation. Wearing a gemstone necklace, earrings, bracelet, or ring to embrace the power of your chosen
archetype is just plain magic.

8

Mantras
The Power of the Spoken Word

Your thoughts are one of your most powerful and magical tools. What you think, speak, and believe becomes your reality. Your thoughts can help propel you forward or they can stop you dead in your tracks. I think back to the time when I separated from my first husband. I was a single mother of a teenager and I had never really been out on my own before. I thought to myself, "Wow, this is going to be hard. This is going to be a difficult journey, but I will make it." Well, that is exactly what it was: a difficult journey, and I made it. What if I had changed my perspective and thought something like, "Wow, I have the freedom to become me now and I have the power to create my success story. Now we will be better off and we can welcome new growth and potential." What would have happened then? Would I have started a new path full of freedom and new beginnings? What if I had embraced the energy of the Fool rather than being bound by the Devil?

Now when I have a negative thought, I use the words *clear, erase, delete* and I replace the negative thought with positive words. I literally speak the new positive thought out loud in the form of words. This changes the energy and produces a positive outcome.

Thoughts are powerful all by themselves, but when you add the magic of the voice, of sound, you increase the power of your thoughts exponentially. Thoughts belong to you. They only live within you, but they do live because you bring them to life. You thought them. You created that thought, whether it is positive or negative. Whether it is encouraging or debilitating, you created it. This thought can and will affect you in some manner, either now or in the future, if not replaced by a positive thought process. Our negative thoughts can become self-fulfilling prophecies if we let them.

When shifting personal energies, we are setting our intentions and petitioning the universe, god, goddess, or archetype of our choice for assistance in the matter at hand. By creating a mantra and speaking this mantra out loud, we are adding a new vibrational element or tool: the magical tool of sound.

A mantra is a sacred sound, syllable, word, or combination of words that is spoken in repetition in order to call in spiritual, magical, or religious energies or powers. The word OM is often spoken to open and close ceremonies. This word represents the sound of the universe. Here we are welcoming the gift of pure potential from the universe.

Think of how sound has been used throughout time. We offer up our gratitude, rejoice, and pray in song, poem, and spoken word. We are able to express our feelings and emotions through our words. Music, a beautiful form of sound, can affect how we are feeling. Music can cheer us up and music can make us cry. We are able to communicate openly and outwardly with the power of sound. We celebrate through song on our special occasions such as birthdays and holidays. Monks chant and choirs sing and pray in gratitude. We ask for support through prayer. Herein lies the power: we must ask for what we want and need in our lives. Our angels, guides, and even the universe must have our permission in order to be of service to us. We must ask.

So how do we create our own mantras? We start with our intention and our chosen archetypal energy. Let's say you are in your Strength year. The situation at hand calls for you to be strong and grounded no matter what is going on around you. The Strength card tells you that you really need to trust in yourself and your decisions. To create your mantra, first you would pull out the keywords for your card. With the Strength card, we have words such as compassion, unconditional love, strength, courage, trust, fortitude, and owning all your parts, the shadow and the light. Your mantra may be something like this:

I am strong and centered in my being. I trust my decisions and I know what is right for me. I open my heart to compassion and unconditional love. I move forward with courage.

Let's look at the same situation using a different card. You are in your Strength year and you have decided to work with the Star during this time to call in hope and a sense of well-being. I think of the keywords for the Star as hope, inspiration, well-being, guidance, and the opportunity to shine for others. So your mantra may be as follows:

My heart is hopeful for the future. I am inspired by the support I feel within, and I am open to receive guidance from the universe as to my next direction. I shine bright with hope and joy, and others are inspired by my internal light.

Now that you have your mantra, you would want to speak it out loud to the universe at a minimum of three times per day. Remember that this mantra is calling in knowledge and new energies to support you on your path forward. Be proud of who you are and where you are going. You are powerful and deserving of your true identity.

By honing in on your intention and using a mantra to let the universe know your desired path, you have opened up the energy of potential. You have called in support from your guides, angels, and your chosen archetype. You are open and willing to receive. By stating your intention through a mantra and reciting your mantra three times daily, you have created ritual.

9

Creating Simple
Everyday Ritual

Magic is born through the power of intention combined with ritual. We are creatures of habit, and we all have daily rituals that make up our day-to-day life. Getting up in the morning and heading straight to the coffee pot is a ritual. Brushing your teeth before bed, dinner at 6 p.m., or saying a nighttime prayer are all rituals. Magic is born through the power of the intention behind the ritual. Once we have our intention in place, the ritual creates the reminder, the memory, and therefore becomes the voice for the intention. Intention is thought, and ritual is action. We can think of ritual as the act of nurturing the intention into fruition.

As we would water our garden, we water and nourish our intention through ritual. In this chapter we will discuss simple rituals that you can personally create to call in the power and support of the universe and hone your personal strength, courage, and determination to manifest your intention into reality. By setting an intention, you hold the key to success within your hands. Ritual is the action of unlocking the door.

Intention

We must have an intention for our ritual. Remember to allow yourself to see the big picture before creating the detail. Once your intention has been defined, the rest is easy. Your path forward has been lit by the light of your intention, and now you can create the street signs that keep you on your path through the reminder of everyday ritual.

Ritual

Rituals can be small and simple or grand and large. I prefer to work with smaller, shorter rituals every day. This is why aromatherapy is a powerful tool for magic. Scents distort time; they can bring back memories and craft new ones. When working with an oil, I like to breathe in the scent or place the oil upon my body a minimum of three times per day. If you look at the number three and its counterpart, the Empress, you will see the power of three. The number three is growth from the one and the two. So with the power of three, we have the number one and manifestation, the Magician; the number two and internal knowing, intuition, the power of decision, and the High Priestess; as well as the number three, the Empress, with the powers of growth, abundance, grounding, and fertility. We are working with a large crew here to support us.

I pair the scent with my vision of success so that when I smell the oil, I know it is manifesting for me and I remember my intention and goal with the scent.

Working with an essential oil is just one form of ritual. We will discuss some additional forms of ritual as we move through this chapter.

Mantra

A mantra is a word or phrase spoken over and over again. It is usually paired with meditation. However, mantra is a very powerful magical tool because words contain power. What we speak and believe becomes our reality. Belief is another key to working successful magic.

Your mantras don't need to be complex. Let's say you are starting a new business and you really want a firm foundation for your business as well as growth and success. You could use this as a mantra: "I am grounded, centered and in balance. I have created a firm foundation of growth and success for my business." Breathe in your oil and repeat the mantra three times per day. This is how I began my journey with mantra through working with essential oils. I am no longer the person I was eight years ago. That's the power of magic.

Cooking

Cooking and eating are other potent forms of magic. I love the idea of adding spices to your cooking with intention. Maybe you desire more passion in your life? A dash of garlic, cayenne, or ginger to a dish brings in a bit more fire. Let's bring that fire into your life and set the intention to bring more passion and desire to your world. I once heard the magical Rana George mention that she likes to add rose water to her dishes. She does this to call more love into her family and sweeten the moods of certain family members. Rose water helps open the heart chakra. Bay laurel can be added for family protection. There are so many choices. Just add your spice with intention.

Creating an Altar

Working with an altar is another way to call in magic. Creating an altar for your chosen tarot energy and placing all the elemental energies that this card represents upon your altar is key. If you're working with a fire element such as the Strength card, then placing a fire oil upon the altar along with candles, a cauldron, spices such as black pepper, or even a tea such as ginger could all be used. Of course you would also want the Strength card on your altar.

The altar is a sacred space that you create to help manifest your intention. This sacred space is a place where you can visually see and be reminded daily of your intention. The altar is also a space to give thanks to your archetype and the universe for assisting in your journey.

The altar sets up a place for you to do your daily rituals. Lighting candles will call in the power of fire. Inhalation of your chosen scent creates a scent memory of your intention and calls in the plant spirit for assistance, and a mantra allows you to redirect your thoughts, shifting them in a positive manner, therefore allowing for the creation of your intention. By reciting your mantra out loud, you are sending your vibrations up to the universe, where your intention is heard and recognized.

Teas

Creating and drinking herbal teas as well as working with black, green, white, and red teas with intention behind their blend is very powerful magic. Choose the herbs that support your elemental energy, such as lavender for the air element, and create your blend. The magic not only lies in the blend that you create but also the ritual you create for the tea. I like to sit in the morning with my tea and feel my hands around the cup. Here I not only feel the warmth and comfort that this tea, this gift, is providing, but I allow myself to envision as well as verbally request my desired outcome in the form of a prayer or mantra. I say my mantra or my desires into the cup, again envisioning the whole, and then I drink the tea and the prayer into my being. In this way, not only have I verbalized my intention and desires, I now also embody them. I become more focused and open to create me and who I wish to become. Tea is magic.

EARTHY TEAS: Roobios, honeybush

WATER TEAS: Green teas

FIRE TEAS: Black teas

AIR TEAS: White teas

Ritual Baths

We often think of baths as purifying and cleansing, but ritual baths can clear one's aura as well as create a magical cauldron of which you are a part of. Herbal baths are lovely and relaxing. For herbal baths I recommend purchasing a bath bag and placing your herbs in this bag prior to placing it in the bath water so your herbs will not go all over the bath and make a mess for you to clean up. You can also add crystals of your choice directly into the herbal bag. You can make an herbal tea to add to your bath water, such as a really strong chamomile tea. Allow the tea to cool and then add directly into your bath water. I also recommend purchasing some Dead Sea salt as well as some Epsom salts. Use about ½ cup of each into a one cup container and then add into your bath. Put any essential oils that you wish to add to your bath directly into 1 tablespoon of jojoba oil and then add into the bath water. If you do not have jojoba oil, when added to the bath water, the essential oils will just stick to the sides of the tub. The jojoba is your carrier for the essential oils, and the salts help remove toxins from the body.

If you do not have a bathtub, you can easily create a shower scrub to work with. Use one cup of Dead Sea salts. Place your essential oils in about ½ cup of carrier oil and then add the combination of carrier oil and essential oils to the cup of salt. You will not need to fill the whole container with the carrier oil; just add enough to make the salts wet and usable. Scrub the salt blend upon your body in the shower. Do not use a salt scrub after shaving. If you have sensitive skin, you can use sugar instead of salt.

Colors and Stones

Wearing the colors of the elemental energy that you are embracing is very magical. Not only will the colors you choose affect your mood and energy, they will also affect those around you. The color red instills courage, passion, and confidence. Blue instills a cool and calm energy, and green is earthy, grounding, and calls in growth and abundance. Black is for protection, and pink is for heart energy and love. I like to choose a tarot card to work with and then wear the colors, use an essential oil that relates to the element, and walk the walk as well as talk the talk. I choose my jewelry very carefully, intentionally wearing a stone with the energy of the element that I am currently working with.

Part Three

What's Next?

10

Expanding the Tarot Apothecary Approach

The tarot apothecary approach can be used to work with your community, family, or for the world at large. You can use this approach to be of service to the world by creating a ritual of support, or you can use this approach to become more involved and possibly become a leader in your chosen area of knowledge. It is totally up to you.

Maybe you are concerned with the world's climate. You personally want to send out some magical energy to help call attention to climate change. Of course, first you must get clear on your intention. You personally work very hard to do your part with climate change. You do everything you can at home to support change, yet you are not a speaker and you are not one to go out and demonstrate or lead your community in any form. You wish to help spiritually: this is your intention. You wish to create a beam of light that radiates out into the world. This light speaks of purification, clarity, compassion, and hope. Look at the keywords that have been chosen. Here I see the energies of water (purification and compassion) and air (clarity and hope).

The first card I would pull out of my deck as the main card for this magical working would be the World card. This is your center card for your altar. This is the subject of your intention. Now take a look at those keywords again. Which major arcana cards or members of the Council of Queens do you wish to work with? Remember that we are working with the elements of water and air. Who in the tarot do you wish to be represented by in this process? Which characteristics do you personally wish to embrace to help in the matter at hand? Maybe you wish to call in the energies of the Star for hope since you personally want to represent hope in the world. Remember that by becoming the Star, you are hope; you will radiate light from within your being. You will be seen by others as a ray of hope. This would allow you to speak with friends and family about the climate and draw them in with your powerful light energy.

Now, who else would you like to support you along the way? Since you are working with the word *clarity*, you could possibly call in the Queen of Swords (air). She may not be emotional in character, but she will make things clear and be truthful and fair. She will get things in order and done. The Queen of Swords also does well with communication; maybe she will call in your communication skills. Maybe you start writing or blogging about the environment, therefore allowing your own voice to be heard.

As a last support card, you could call in the Queen of Cups for your water element energy. This queen is compassionate, and her heart is open. She will start the flow outward and help you listen to your intuition. This queen will be of service and open the hearts of others.

Another option for personal representation could be the Empress, who would nurture the earth with healing. Maybe you want to manifest change; then you could choose the Magician. There are many options.

Now let's take a look at our chosen cards and their essential oil companions. We have the World in the center of your altar. This is the subject of the story or magical working. We are using sandalwood for the World, so place your bottle of sandalwood in front of your World card. For the Star we have violet absolute. For the Queen of Swords, you could use any air oil, such as peppermint, rosemary, lemongrass, eucalyptus, lavender, etc. For the Queen of Cups, any water elemental oils such as lemon balm, rose, ylang-ylang, etc. Place your chosen oils upon the altar in front of their tarot companions. You can choose to create a blend or work with each oil individually.

For ritual, maybe you sit in meditation with each card individually and work with the essential oil, choosing one card each day of the week to work with. Maybe you do a different ritual for each card, dancing for the World, sending out light energy for the Star, writing or blogging for the Queen of Swords, and taking a ritual bath for the Queen of Cups. There are many options. The key here is intention and action. Creating a healing and purifying mantra to work with daily in support of the climate would allow your intention to be heard by the universe.

This is just one example of calling in energy for the World using the tarot apothecary approach.

Working with Your Community

Helping your community through the tarot apothecary approach is magic. Let's say you have been chosen to do some fundraising for the new community center that your town is building. The plans have been drawn up and the land has been bought. The building will be going up soon, but the community could use some help with furnishing the new building. Since this is a community center, there are many needed supplies. So your first step is to set your intention, which is to raise as much money as you can for furniture and supplies for the new building. Who would you choose in the tarot to represent you as the leader in this challenge? Maybe the Emperor? Think of the Emperor's power. The Emperor is fire element. He is the spark that gets the flame going. He is leadership, power, structure, a powerful delegator, and the father figure; what a great combination to create your desired outcome. You can lead now and delegate powers to others, who now can become your team members. You become the spark, and you carry the power to lead the way. The essential oil for the Emperor is oakwood absolute. Think of the power of the mighty oak: its strength, its structure, and its power to create and protect. You have all you need to be powerful for those who need you to lead the way.

To support your Emperor power, you decide to work with the Queen of Pentacles. The Queen of Pentacles will lay a foundation for your work and call in a grounding effect to the Emperor's flame. The Emperor may get bored with the project and want to move on to something more exciting. The Queen of Pentacles will not allow this. She will keep you centered and moving in the right direction. You can choose any of the earthy essential oils to work with for this amazing queen.

Another example may be that you have personally decided to become a leader for your daughter's Brownie troop. What an undertaking! Your intention is to teach and support these young ladies to help them grow up to be strong and secure young women. You have chosen to work with the Empress, the nurturing mother. She has knowledge and loves nature. She is caring and brings growth and abundance to all who work with her. What a great foundation for leading a group of children. The Empress's essential oil is patchouli, which is playful and fun and asks you to dance and enjoy life. You will share this energy with your troop.

For support, you choose to work with the Sun. The Sun is masculine energy to help to balance the feminine energy of the Empress. The Sun is joy, happiness, and fun. This allows you to nurture and bring joy into the hearts of your Brownie troop and teach them about individuality. You support each child in being themselves. The essential oil for the Sun is orange oil, whether you choose to work with sweet orange oil, neroli, or petitgrain. Make an orange spritzer to spray and share with your troop. It will uplift their hearts, minds, and emotional bodies.

There are so many different and powerful ways to work with the cards to bring support and magic to your community and the world you live in. You have the power within you to create whatever it is that you desire to be true for you and the world around you. Although things do not always happen on your timeline or in the manner that you may imagine, you will reach someone; you will touch someone and inspire that someone to make the change they currently need in their life. You will make the changes you need in your life. Through helping others, you will grow and expand your energy, and you will be another step closer to creating your chosen reality.

11

Introducing the Tarot Apothecary Approach to Others

As I mentioned before, you do not need to be a tarot pro or even a tarot reader to use and work with the tarot apothecary. This approach is for everyone. In this manner you can help friends and family find out who they are in the tarot and what year they are currently in. You can help them take the next step on their path. You can help them discover and work toward their intended goal.

Often we as individuals do not know who we are, where we wish to go, or who we wish to become in life. This is not uncommon. It wasn't until I discovered who I was in the tarot that I began to understand myself and my skills and trust my desires. I needed some grounding to build upon. I found that grounding through the tarot apothecary. You can do the same for yourself and others.

Let's look at an example. Your mom is retiring from her thirty-five-year profession as a school teacher. She is ready for rest and to really take time for herself now. She wants to embrace her individuality and maybe pick up a hobby or a skill that she can possibly sell or share with her family. She is totally unaware of what to do. Well, you can take it from here.

Your first step is to talk to your mom and find out what she is thinking. Does she have any specific plans or desires? If she is unclear, that is totally fine. This is part of the equation, helping bring clarity to the picture as a whole. Another great way to start this is to have your mom write down her desires. If she could have any life she wanted right now, what would that look like? What would she be doing? Where would she live? What would stay the same in her life, and what would change? What challenges could possibly pop up? These are all great questions to discuss and work through.

Once you have some form of direction, you can start the process. First and foremost, who is your mom in the tarot? What are her skills and challenges based on her personal tarot archetype?

Next, what year is your mom currently in? This is the key for movement forward. What are the challenges and gifts of this particular year? What are the keywords for the year card? How can she use this year's energies for advancement toward her goal?

Let's say that your mom is the Empress in the tarot. She is a nurturer and really wants to nurture herself for a change. After looking at her list of things she would like to incorporate into her life, she has decided that she wants to embrace cooking. Through cooking she can nurture her family and friends, and she can nurture herself through the gift of creating. She loves Italian and Greek food; maybe she could take some cooking classes or travel and taste the foods and experience the life and culture that lives in the food.

After calculating your mom's tarot year numerology, you discover that your mom is in her Death year. That makes total sense. The Death year is about transformation and change, letting go of the old to create the new. Your mom is retiring and letting go of her old career and many of the friends she has made along the way. Some friends will stay and some will eventually go. She is in a huge transformation. What a great time to embrace self. Now your mom can look at the energies that are surrounding her and make a decision.

Let's look at the whole picture here. Your mom is the Empress in the tarot, and she is currently in her Death year. She has decided that she wants to do both travel and courses on cooking. Are there any obstacles? Maybe she will need to set aside some money and save more to start her travel, but she can start some courses right away. Maybe she will find some friends to travel with in her classes or maybe there will be a trip already planned through the school. She will start with the courses. This is her first step forward.

The next step for you in the equation would be to see if a companion card or supporting card is wanted or needed. To save her money, maybe you suggest working with the Queen of Pentacles. This queen will help create new ground and save the funds needed for travel. Maybe you have her embrace the World card. Your mom has completed one phase of her life and is moving into another. She has the World at her feet and can start creating her new life. Maybe you have her embrace the Fool card. The Fool would allow her to feel her freedom and take the leap of faith into the next phase of her life. You can now help her create a mantra and then choose ritual and oils for her to work with in order to move forward.

You have created a plan for success and helped your mom move forward with less stress and worry. She has the power to re-create herself and her life into the life she now chooses. She is grateful for your insight and help.

The tarot apothecary is a magical approach that allows for self-development and success. Now that you have charted your path forward, you can now do this for others. Just re-create the worksheet in the book for each person that you work with and use this as your guide for yourself and others.

Final Thoughts

The tarot apothecary has been a magical discovery in my life. I have learned more about my personal skills and the challenges I may face in life. I have learned how to ask for support in times of need, and I have created a web of resources for my magical cauldron through working with the tarot, aromatherapy, imaginative journey, and ritual. I bring my discoveries to you in hopes that you, too, will learn more about yourself and gain the wisdom and courage to create your true being. I hope that you take this knowledge and help others discover who they truly are and who they truly wish to become in life.

I ask you to challenge yourself and learn from the energy of the cards and your life experiences. Take this knowledge with you as you journey into self-discovery and healing for yourself and your friends, family, community, and the world at large.

You are magic. Know this.

Appendix

Essential Oils

||||||||||||

For all essential oils, keep away from children and do not use on children. Check precautions prior to making and using any blends due to possible skin irritations, and always dilute essential oils with a carrier oil before any contact with skin. For more detailed information before usage, see https://www.takingcharge.csh.umn.edu /are-essential-oils-safe.

Agarwood (*Aquilaria crassna Pierre ex Lecomte*)
ELEMENT: Earth
PLANT PART: Wood
BLENDING NOTE: Base
SCENT GROUP: Woody
PLANT FAMILY: Thymelaeaceae
EXTRACTION METHOD: Hydrodistillation
PRECAUTIONS: Keep away from children.

Amyris (*Amyris balsamifera*)
ELEMENT: Earth
PLANT PART: Wood, bark
BLENDING NOTE: Base
SCENT GROUP: Woody

PLANT FAMILY: Rutaceae
EXTRACTION METHOD: Steam distillation
PRECAUTIONS: Keep away from children.

Angelica Root *(Angelica archangelica)*

ELEMENT: Earth
PLANT PART: Root
BLENDING NOTE: Base, middle
SCENT GROUP: Herbaceous
PLANT FAMILY: Apieceae
EXTRACTION METHOD: Steam distillation
PRECAUTIONS: Do not use during pregnancy or when nursing. May be phototoxic; avoid sun exposure. Keep away from children.

Angelica Seed *(Angelica archangelica)*

ELEMENT: Fire
PLANT PART: Seed
BLENDING NOTE: Middle, top
SCENT GROUP: Herbaceous
PLANT FAMILY: Apiaceae
EXTRACTION METHOD: Steam distillation
PRECAUTIONS: Not for use with pregnancy or nursing. Avoid if taking diabetic medications. Keep away from children.

Anise *(Pimpinella anisum)*

ELEMENT: Fire
PLANT PART: Seed
BLENDING NOTE: Top
SCENT GROUP: Spicy
PLANT FAMILY: Apiaceae
EXTRACTION METHOD: Steam distillation
PRECAUTIONS: Not for use on children under the age of five. Not for use when taking diabetic medications. Not for use during pregnancy or when

nursing. May be a skin irritant. Always dilute with carrier oil. Avoid use with history of endometriosis or estrogen dependent cancer. Avoid if taking anticoagulant medications; may inhibit blood clotting. Keep away from children.

Basil *(Ocimum basilicum)*

ELEMENT: Fire

PLANT PART: Leaves, flowering tops

BLENDING NOTE: Middle, top

SCENT GROUP: Herbaceous

PLANT FAMILY: Lamiaceae

EXTRACTION METHOD: Steam distillation

PRECAUTIONS: May be skin irritant. Always dilute with carrier oil. Do not use in bath. Not for use on children under the age of five. Do not use if taking diabetic medications. Not for use during pregnancy or when nursing. Considered mildly toxic and possibly carcinogenic. Avoid if taking anticoagulant medications. Keep away from children.

Benzoin *(Styrax benzoin)*

ELEMENT: Earth, air

PLANT PART: Resin, gum

BLENDING NOTE: Base, middle

SCENT GROUP: Spicy

PLANT FAMILY: Styracaceae

EXTRACTION METHOD: Solvent extraction

PRECAUTIONS: May cause skin irritation. Always dilute prior to use. Do not use in bath. Not for use on children under the age of five.

Bergamot *(Citrus bergamia)*

ELEMENT: Fire

PLANT PART: Fruit peel (rind)

BLENDING NOTE: Top

Scent Group: Citrus

Plant Family: Rutaceae

Extraction Method: Cold pressed

Precautions: May be a skin irritant. Always dilute with carrier oil. Do not use in bath. May be phototoxic; avoid sun exposure. Keep away from children.

Bergamot Mint *(Mentha citrata)*

Element: Air

Plant Part: Leaves

Blending Note: Middle, top

Scent Group: Herbaceous

Plant Family: Lamiaceae

Extraction Method: Steam distillation

Precautions: Do not use in bath. Keep away from children.

Black Pepper *(Piper nigrum)*

Element: Fire

Plant Part: Unripe peppercorns (fruit)

Blending Note: Base, middle

Scent Group: Spicy

Plant Family: Piperaceae

Extraction Method: Steam distillation

Precautions: May be a skin irritant. Always dilute with carrier oil. Do not use in bath. Not recommended for use when taking homeopathic medications. Not for long-term use. Do not use for more than ten days in a row. Keep away from children.

Caraway Seed *(Carum carvi)*

Element: Fire

Plant Part: Seeds

Blending Note: Middle

SCENT GROUP: Spicy

PLANT FAMILY: Apiaceae

EXTRACTION METHOD: Steam distillation

PRECAUTIONS: Do not use oil if oxidized. Keep away from children.

Cardamom *(Elettaria cardamomum)*

ELEMENT: Water

PLANT PART: Seeds

BLENDING NOTE: Middle

SCENT GROUP: Spicy

PLANT FAMILY: Zingiberaceae

EXTRACTION METHOD: Steam distillation

PRECAUTIONS: Not for use on children under the age of five.

Cassia *(Cinnamomum cassia)*

ELEMENT: Fire

PLANT PART: Bark

BLENDING NOTE: Top

SCENT GROUP: Spicy

PLANT FAMILY: Lauraceae

EXTRACTION METHOD: Steam distillation

PRECAUTIONS: May be skin irritant. Always dilute with carrier oil. Do not use in bath. Not for use on children under the age of five. Do not use when taking diabetic medications. Not for use during pregnancy or when nursing. Not for use when taking anticoagulant medications. May inhibit blood clotting. Keep away from children.

Catnip *(Nepeta cataria)*

ELEMENT: Air

PLANT PART: Flowering tops

BLENDING NOTE: Middle, top

SCENT GROUP: Herbaceous
PLANT FAMILY: Lamiaceae
EXTRACTION METHOD: Steam distillation
PRECAUTIONS: May be skin irritant. Always dilute
  with carrier oil. Do not use in bath. Keep away from
  children.

Virginia cedarwood (*Juniperus virginiana*)
ELEMENT: Earth, fire, air
PLANT PART: Wood, bark
BLENDING NOTE: Base, middle
SCENT GROUP: Woody
PLANT FAMILY: Cupressaceae
EXTRACTION METHOD: Steam distillation
PRECAUTIONS: Keep away from children.

Cinnamon
(*Cinnamomum verum/Cinnamomum zeylanicum) Bark oil*
ELEMENT: Fire
PLANT PART: Bark
BLENDING NOTE: Middle
SCENT GROUP: Spicy
PLANT FAMILY: Lauraceae
EXTRACTION METHOD: Steam distillation
PRECAUTIONS: May be skin irritant. Always dilute
  with carrier oil. Do not use in bath. Not for use
  on children under the age of five. Not for use with
  pregnancy or when nursing. Considered moderately
  toxic and possibly carcinogenic. Do not use if
  taking anticoagulant medications. May inhibit
  blood clotting. Not for use when taking diabetic
  medication. Keep away from children.

Cinnamon Leaf
(*Cinnamomum verum/Cinnamomum zeylanicum*)

ELEMENT: Fire

PLANT PART: Leaves

BLENDING NOTE: Middle

SCENT GROUP: Spicy

PLANT FAMILY: Lauraceae

EXTRACTION METHOD: Steam distillation

PRECAUTIONS: May be skin irritant. Always dilute with carrier oil. Do not use in bath. Not for use on children under the age of five. Not for use when pregnant or nursing. Considered moderately toxic and possibly carcinogenic. Do not use if taking anticoagulant medications. May inhibit blood clotting. Keep away from children.

German Chamomile *(Matricaria recutica)*

ELEMENT: Water

PLANT PART: Flowers

BLENDING NOTE: Base, middle

SCENT GROUP: Floral

PLANT FAMILY: Asteraceae

EXTRACTION METHOD: Steam distillation

PRECAUTIONS: Do not use if taking CYP2D6 medications. Keep away from children. Do not use if you have a ragweed allergy.

Roman Chamomile *(Anthemis nobilis/Chamaemelum nobile)*

ELEMENT: Water

PLANT PART: Flowers

BLENDING NOTE: Middle

SCENT GROUP: Floral

PLANT FAMILY: Asteraceae

EXTRACTION METHOD: Steam distillation

PRECAUTIONS: Keep away from children. Do not use if you have a ragweed allergy.

Citronella *(Cymbopogon nardus)*
ELEMENT: Air

PLANT PART: Leaves

BLENDING NOTE: Top

SCENT GROUP: Herbaceous

PLANT FAMILY: Poaceae

EXTRACTION METHOD: Steam distillation

PRECAUTIONS: Not for use on children under the age of five. Not for use during pregnancy or when nursing. May be a skin irritant. Always dilute with carrier oil. Do not use in bath. Keep away from children.

Clary Sage *(Salvia sclarea)*
ELEMENT: Water

PLANT PART: Leaves, flowering tops

BLENDING NOTE: Base, middle

SCENT GROUP: Herbaceous

PLANT FAMILY: Lamiaceae

EXTRACTION METHOD: Steam distillation

PRECAUTIONS: May increase narcotic effect if drinking alcohol. May cause headache with overuse. Do not use if pregnant or nursing. Keep away from children.

Clove *(Syzygium aromaticum syn Eugenia caryophyllata)*
ELEMENT: Fire

PLANT PART: Flower buds

BLENDING NOTE: Middle

SCENT GROUP: Spicy

PLANT FAMILY: Myrtaceae

EXTRACTION METHOD: Steam distillation

PRECAUTIONS: May be skin irritant. Always dilute with carrier oil. Do not use in bath. Not for use on children under the age of five. Do not use in pregnancy or when nursing. Considered moderately toxic and possibly carcinogenic. Avoid if using anticoagulant medications. May inhibit blood clotting. Keep away from children.

Coriander *(Coriandrum sativum)*
ELEMENT: Fire
PLANT PART: Seed
BLENDING NOTE: Middle
SCENT GROUP: Spicy
PLANT FAMILY: Apiaceae
EXTRACTION METHOD: Steam distillation
PRECAUTIONS: Keep away from children.

Cornmint *(Mentha arvensis)*
ELEMENT: Air
PLANT PART: Leaves
BLENDING NOTE: Top
SCENT GROUP: Herbaceous
PLANT FAMILY: Lamiaceae
EXTRACTION METHOD: Steam distillation
PRECAUTIONS: Do not use if you have cardiac fibrillation and G6PD deficiency. Not for use on children under the age of five. Keep away from children.

Cumin *(Cuminum cyminum)*
ELEMENT: Fire
PLANT PART: Seeds
BLENDING NOTE: Middle
SCENT GROUP: Spicy
PLANT FAMILY: Apiaceae
EXTRACTION METHOD: Steam distillation
PRECAUTIONS: Not for use during pregnancy or nursing. May be phototoxic; avoid sun exposure. Keep away from children.

Cypress *(Cupressus sempervirens)*
ELEMENT: Water, earth
PLANT PART: Needles, twigs, leaves
BLENDING NOTE: Base, middle
SCENT GROUP: Woody
PLANT FAMILY: Cupressaceae
EXTRACTION METHOD: Steam distillation
PRECAUTIONS: Do not use if oxidized. Keep away
from children.

Eucalyptus *(Eucalyptus globules)*
ELEMENT: Air
PLANT PART: Leaves
BLENDING NOTE: Middle, top
SCENT GROUP: Woody
PLANT FAMILY: Myrtaceae
EXTRACTION METHOD: Steam distillation
PRECAUTIONS: Do not use in bath. Not for use on
children under the age of five. Not recommended
for those taking homeopathic remedies. Keep away
from children.

Lemon Eucalyptus *(Eucalyptus citriodora)*
ELEMENT: Air
PLANT PART: Leaves
BLENDING NOTE: Middle, top
SCENT GROUP: Citrus
PLANT FAMILY: Myrtaceae
EXTRACTION METHOD: Steam distillation
PRECAUTIONS: Keep away from children.

Sweet Fennel *(Foeniculum vulgare var. dulce)*
ELEMENT: Fire
PLANT PART: Seeds
BLENDING NOTE: Top
SCENT GROUP: Spicy

PLANT FAMILY: Apiaceae

EXTRACTION METHOD: Steam distillation

PRECAUTIONS: May be skin irritant. Always dilute with carrier oil. Do not use in bath. Not for use on children under the age of five. Not for use when taking diabetic medications. Not for use with epilepsy. Not for long-term use; do not use more than ten days in a row. Not for use during pregnancy or when nursing. Considered moderately toxic and possibly carcinogenic. Avoid with history of endometriosis and estrogen dependent cancer. Do not use when taking anticoagulant medications; may inhibit blood clotting. Keep away from children.

Balsam Fir *(Albie balsamea)*

ELEMENT: Earth, fire, air

PLANT PART: Needles, oleoresin

BLENDING NOTE: Middle

SCENT GROUP: Woody

PLANT FAMILY: Pinaceae

EXTRACTION METHOD: Steam distillation

PRECAUTIONS: Avoid oil if it has oxidized. Keep away from children.

Douglas Fir *(Pseudotsuga menziesii)*

ELEMENT: Earth, fire, air

PLANT PART: Needles, twigs

BLENDING NOTE: Top

SCENT GROUP: Woody

PLANT FAMILY: Pinaceae

EXTRACTION METHOD: Steam distillation

PRECAUTIONS: Do not use once oxidized. Keep away from children.

Silver Fir *(Albies alba)*
ELEMENT: Earth, fire, air
PLANT PART: Needles
BLENDING NOTE: Middle
SCENT GROUP: Woody
PLANT FAMILY: Pinaceae
EXTRACTION METHOD: Steam distillation
PRECAUTIONS: Do not use once oxidized. Keep
away from children.

Frankincense *(Boswellia carteri)*
ELEMENT: Earth, fire
PLANT PART: Oleoresin, resin
BLENDING NOTE: Base
SCENT GROUP: Resinous
PLANT FAMILY: Burseraceae
EXTRACTION METHOD: Steam distillation,
hydrodistillation
PRECAUTIONS: Not for use during pregnancy
or nursing. Avoid if oxidized. Keep away from
children. This oil is phototoxic; avoid sun exposure.

Galangal *(Alpinia officinarum)*
ELEMENT: Earth
PLANT PART: Rhizome
BLENDING NOTE: Middle
SCENT GROUP: Spicy
PLANT FAMILY: Zingiberaceae
EXTRACTION METHOD: Steam distillation
PRECAUTIONS: Always dilute with carrier oil. Keep
away from children.

Ginger *(Zingiber officinale)*
ELEMENT: Fire
PLANT PART: Root

BLENDING NOTE: Middle
SCENT GROUP: Spicy
PLANT FAMILY: Zingiberacea
EXTRACTION METHOD: Steam distillation
PRECAUTIONS: May be skin irritant. Always dilute
    with carrier oil. Do not use in bath. Keep away from
    children.

Grapefruit *(Citrus x paradisi)*

ELEMENT: Water, fire
PLANT PART: Fruit
BLENDING NOTE: Middle, top
SCENT GROUP: Citrus
PLANT FAMILY: Rutaceae
EXTRACTION METHOD: Cold pressed
PRECAUTIONS: May be skin irritant. Always
    dilute with carrier oil. Do not use in bath. May be
    phototoxic; avoid sun exposure. Keep away from
    children.

Ho Wood *(Cinnamomum camphora var linalool)*

ELEMENT: Earth
PLANT PART: Wood
BLENDING NOTE: Middle
SCENT GROUP: Woody
PLANT FAMILY: Lauraceae
EXTRACTION METHOD: Steam distillation
PRECAUTIONS: Keep away from children.

Hyssop *(Hyssopus officinalis var decumbens)*

ELEMENT: Fire
PLANT PART: Leaves, flowering tops
BLENDING NOTE: Top
SCENT GROUP: Herbaceous
PLANT FAMILY: Lamiaceae

EXTRACTION METHOD: Steam distillation

PRECAUTIONS: Not for use on children under the age of five. Not for use with epilepsy. Not recommended for those with high blood pressure. Not for use during pregnancy or when nursing. Keep away from children.

Jasmine Absolute *(Jasminum grandiflorum)*

ELEMENT: Water

PLANT PART: Flowers

BLENDING NOTE: Base, middle

SCENT GROUP: Floral

PLANT FAMILY: Oleaceae

EXTRACTION METHOD: Solvent extraction

PRECAUTIONS: Not for use on children under the age of five. Always dilute with carrier oil. Keep away from children.

Juniper *(Juniperus communis)*

ELEMENT: Earth, fire

PLANT PART: Unripe berries

BLENDING NOTE: Middle

SCENT GROUP: Woody

PLANT FAMILY: Cupressaceae

EXTRACTION METHOD: Steam distillation

PRECAUTIONS: Not for use with kidney disease. Not for long-term use; do not use more than ten days in a row. Keep away from children.

Lavender *(Lavendula angustifolia)*

ELEMENT: Air

PLANT PART: Flowering tops, leaves

BLENDING NOTE: Middle

SCENT GROUP: Floral

PLANT FAMILY: Lamiaceae

EXTRACTION METHOD: Steam distillation
PRECAUTIONS: Keep away from children.

Lemon *(Citrus limon)*

ELEMENT: Water
PLANT PART: Rind
BLENDING NOTE: Top
SCENT GROUP: Citrus
PLANT FAMILY: Rutaceae
EXTRACTION METHOD: Cold pressed
PRECAUTIONS: May be skin irritant. Always dilute with carrier oil. Do not use in bath. May be phototoxic; avoid sun exposure when wearing this oil. Keep away from children.

Lemon Balm/Melissa *(Melissa Officinalis)*

ELEMENT: Water
PLANT PART: Leaves, flowering tops
BLENDING NOTE: Middle
SCENT GROUP: Citrus
PLANT FAMILY: Lamiaceae
EXTRACTION METHOD: Steam distillation
PRECAUTIONS: May be skin irritant. Always dilute with carrier oil. Do not use in bath. Phototoxic; avoid sun exposure when wearing this oil. Not for use on children under the age of five. Do not use when taking diabetic medications. Not for use with pregnancy or nursing. Keep away from children.

Lemongrass *(Cymbopogon citrates)*

ELEMENT: Air
PLANT PART: Leaves
BLENDING NOTE: Middle, top
SCENT GROUP: Citrus
PLANT FAMILY: Poaceae

EXTRACTION METHOD: Steam distillation

PRECAUTIONS: May be skin irritant. Always dilute with carrier oil. Do not use in bath. Not for use on children under the age of five. Do not use if taking diabetic medications. Not for use when pregnant or nursing. Not for use with CYP2B6-tricyclic antidepressants. Keep away from children.

Lime *(Citrus aurantifolia)*

ELEMENT: Fire

PLANT PART: Rind/peel

BLENDING NOTE: Top

SCENT GROUP: Citrus

PLANT FAMILY: Rutaceae

EXTRACTION METHOD: Cold pressed

PRECAUTIONS: May be skin irritant. Always dilute with carrier oil. Do not use in bath. May be phototoxic; avoid sun exposure. Keep away from children.

Mandarin/Tangerine *(Citrus reticulata)*

ELEMENT: Fire

PLANT PART: Rind/peel

BLENDING NOTE: Top

SCENT GROUP: Citrus

PLANT FAMILY: Rutaceae

EXTRACTION METHOD: Cold pressed

PRECAUTIONS: May be skin irritant. Always dilute with carrier oil. Do not use in bath. May be phototoxic; avoid sun exposure. Keep away from children.

Marjoram *(Origanum marjorana)*

ELEMENT: Air

PLANT PART: Leaves, flowers

BLENDING NOTE: Middle

SCENT GROUP: Herbaceous

PLANT FAMILY: Lamiaceae

EXTRACTION METHOD: Steam distillation

PRECAUTIONS: Do not use when pregnant or nursing. Do not use in bath. Not for long-term use; do not use more than ten days in a row. Keep away from children.

Myrrh *(Commiphora myrrha)*

ELEMENT: Water

PLANT PART: Resin

BLENDING NOTE: Base

SCENT GROUP: Resinous

PLANT FAMILY: Burseraceae

EXTRACTION METHOD: Steam distillation

PRECAUTIONS: Do not use if pregnant or nursing. Always dilute with carrier oil. Keep away from children.

Myrtle *(Myrtus communis)*

ELEMENT: Water

PLANT PART: Leaves

BLENDING NOTE: Middle, top

SCENT GROUP: Herbaceous

PLANT FAMILY: Myrtaceae

EXTRACTION METHOD: Steam distillation

PRECAUTIONS: Do not use if taking diabetic medications. Moderately toxic; may be carcinogenic. Always dilute with carrier oil. Keep away from children.

Neroli *(Citrus aurantium)*

ELEMENT: Water

PLANT PART: Flowers

BLENDING NOTE: Middle

SCENT GROUP: Floral

PLANT FAMILY: Rutaceae

EXTRACTION METHOD: Steam distillation

PRECAUTIONS: Always dilute with carrier oil. Keep away from children.

Nutmeg *(Myristica fragrans)*

ELEMENT: Fire

PLANT PART: Seed

BLENDING NOTE: Middle

SCENT GROUP: Spicy

PLANT FAMILY: Myristicaceae

EXTRACTION METHOD: Steam distillation

PRECAUTIONS: May be skin irritant. Always dilute with carrier oil. Do not use in bath. Not for use on children under the age of five. Not for use during pregnancy or when nursing. Considered moderately toxic and possibly carcinogenic. Keep away from children.

Oakmoss *(Evernia prunastri)*

ELEMENT: Earth

PLANT PART: Moss/lichen

BLENDING NOTE: Base

SCENT GROUP: Woody

PLANT FAMILY: Parmeliaceae

EXTRACTION METHOD: Solvent extraction

PRECAUTIONS: May be sensitizing. Avoid if you have sensitive skin. Always dilute with carrier oil. Not for use on children under the age of five.

Oakwood Absolute *(Quercus robur)*

ELEMENT: Earth

PLANT PART: Wood

BLENDING NOTE: Base

SCENT GROUP: Woody

FAMILY: Beech

EXTRACTION METHOD: Solvent extraction

PRECAUTIONS: Can be a skin irritant. Do not use in bath. Always dilute with carrier oil. Keep away from children. Never take internally. Do not use during pregnancy or when nursing.

Sweet Orange *(Citrus sinensis syn. C. dulcis)*

ELEMENT: Fire

PLANT PART: Rind/peel

BLENDING NOTE: Top

SCENT GROUP: Citrus

PLANT FAMILY: Rutaceae

EXTRACTION METHOD: Cold pressed

PRECAUTIONS: May be skin irritant. Always dilute with carrier oil. Do not use in bath. May be phototoxic; avoid sun exposure. Keep away from children.

Oregano *(Origanum vulgare)*

ELEMENT: Fire, air

PLANT PART: Flowers, leaves

BLENDING NOTE: Middle

SCENT GROUP: Herbaceous

PLANT FAMILY: Lamiaceae

EXTRACTION METHOD: Steam distillation

PRECAUTIONS: May be skin irritant. Always dilute with carrier oil. Do not use in bath. Not for use on children under the age of five. Not for use during pregnancy or when nursing. Do not use with anticoagulant medications. May inhibit blood clotting. Keep away from children.

Palmarosa *(Cymbopogon martinii)*

ELEMENT: Water

PLANT PART: Leaves

BLENDING NOTE: Middle

SCENT GROUP: Floral

PLANT FAMILY: Poaceae

EXTRACTION METHOD: Steam distillation

PRECAUTIONS: Not for use with CYP2B6
medications or tricyclic antidepressants. Always
dilute with carrier oil. Keep away from children.

Parsley *(Petroselinum sativum)*

ELEMENT: Air

PLANT PART: Seeds

BLENDING NOTE: Middle

SCENT GROUP: Herbaceous

PLANT FAMILY: Lamiaceae

EXTRACTION METHOD: Steam distillation

PRECAUTIONS: Not for use with kidney disease.
Do not use if pregnant or nursing. Keep away from
children.

Patchouli *(Pogostemon cablin)*

ELEMENT: Earth

PLANT PART: Leaves

BLENDING NOTE: Base

SCENT GROUP: Woody

PLANT FAMILY: Lamiaceae

EXTRACTION METHOD: Steam distillation

PRECAUTIONS: Do not use with anticoagulant
medications; may inhibit blood clotting. Check
with physician if having surgery. Keep away from
children. Patchouli may cause a skin irritation, so
always dilute it with a carrier oil. Do a skin test
prior to use. Avoid during pregnancy.

Palo Santo *(Bursera graveolens)*

ELEMENT: Earth

PLANT PART: Wood

BLENDING NOTE: Middle

SCENT GROUP: Woody

PLANT FAMILY: Burseraceae

EXTRACTION METHOD: Steam distillation

PRECAUTIONS: May be skin irritant. Always dilute with carrier oil. Avoid use of oil if it has oxidized. Keep away from children.

Peppermint *(Mentha piperita)*

ELEMENT: Air

PLANT PART: Leaves, flowers

BLENDING NOTE: Top

SCENT GROUP: Herbaceous

PLANT FAMILY: Lamiaceae

EXTRACTION METHOD: Steam distillation

PRECAUTIONS: May be skin irritant. Always dilute with carrier oil. Do not use in bath. Not for use on children under the age of five. Not recommended for use with homeopathic remedies. Not for use with pregnancy or nursing. Do not use if taking 5-fluorouracil (an anti-cancer drug) or cyclosporine. Keep away from children.

Petitgrain *(Citrus aurantium)*

ELEMENT: Fire

PLANT PART: Leaves, twigs

BLENDING NOTE: Top

SCENT GROUP: Spicy

PLANT FAMILY: Rutaceae

EXTRACTION METHOD: Steam distillation

PRECAUTIONS: May be skin irritant. Always dilute with carrier oil. Do not use in bath. May be phototoxic; avoid sun exposure. Keep away from children.

Pine *(Pinus sylvestris)*

ELEMENT: Earth

PLANT PART: Needles, twigs

BLENDING NOTE: Middle, top

SCENT GROUP: Woody

PLANT FAMILY: Pinaceae

EXTRACTION METHOD: Steam distillation

PRECAUTIONS: May be a skin irritant. Always dilute
with carrier oil. Do not use in bath. Keep away from
children.

Rose Absolute *(Rosa damascena)*

ELEMENT: Water

PLANT PART: Flowers

BLENDING NOTE: Middle

SCENT GROUP: Floral

PLANT FAMILY: Rosaceae

EXTRACTION METHOD: Solvent extraction

PRECAUTIONS: Always dilute with a carrier oil.

Rose Geranium *(Pelargonium graveolens)*

ELEMENT: Water

PLANT PART: Leaves, stems, flowering tops

BLENDING NOTE: Middle

SCENT GROUP: Floral

PLANT FAMILY: Geraniaceae

EXTRACTION METHOD: Steam distillation

PRECAUTIONS: Not for use on children under
the age of five. Do not use if taking diabetic
medications. May be a skin irritant. Always
dilute with carrier oil. Do not use with CYP2B6
medications, Tricyclic antidepressants, or diabetic
medications. Keep away from children.

Rosemary *(Rosmarinus officinalis)*

ELEMENT: Fire, air

PLANT PART: Leaves, flowering tops

BLENDING NOTE: Middle, top

SCENT GROUP: Herbaceous

PLANT FAMILY: Lamiaceae

EXTRACTION METHOD: Steam distillation

PRECAUTIONS: May be skin irritant. Always dilute with carrier oil. Not for use in bath. Not for use on children under the age of five. Not for use with epilepsy. Not recommended for those taking homeopathic medications. Not for use during pregnancy or nursing. Keep away from children.

Spanish Sage *(Salvia lavandulifolia)*

ELEMENT: Earth, air

PLANT PART: Leaves

BLENDING NOTE: Middle

SCENT GROUP: Herbaceous

PLANT FAMILY: Lamiaceae

EXTRACTION METHOD: Steam distillation

PRECAUTIONS: May be skin irritant. Always dilute with carrier oil. Do not use in bath. Do not use when pregnant or nursing. Not for use on children under the age of five. Not recommended for those with high blood pressure. Keep away from children. Not for use with epilepsy. Avoid use with endometriosis and estrogen dependent cancer. Do not use if taking CYP substrates.

Australian Sandalwood *(Santalum spicatum)*

ELEMENT: Earth, water, air

PLANT PART: Root, heartwood

BLENDING NOTE: Base

SCENT GROUP: Woody
PLANT FAMILY: Santalaceae
EXTRACTION METHOD: Steam distillation
PRECAUTIONS: May be a skin irritant. Always dilute
with carrier oil. Keep away from children.

Spearmint *(Mentha spicata, syn. M. viridis)*
ELEMENT: Air
PLANT PART: Leaves, flowering tops
BLENDING NOTE: Top
SCENT GROUP: Herbaceous
PLANT FAMILY: Lamiaceae
EXTRACTION METHOD: Steam distillation
PRECAUTIONS: May be skin irritant. Always
dilute with carrier oil. Do not use in bath. Not
recommended for use with homeopathic remedies.
Keep away from children.

Spruce *(Pinus canadensis syn. Tsuga canadensis)*
ELEMENT: Earth
PLANT PART: Needles, twigs
BLENDING NOTE: Top
SCENT GROUP: Woody
PLANT FAMILY: Pinaceae
EXTRACTION METHOD: Steam distillation
PRECAUTIONS: May be skin irritant. Always dilute
with carrier oil. Keep away from children.

Tarragon *(Artemisia dracunculus)*
ELEMENT: Fire, air
PLANT PART: Leaves
BLENDING NOTE: Middle
SCENT GROUP: Spicy
PLANT FAMILY: Asteraceae
EXTRACTION METHOD: Steam distillation

PRECAUTIONS: May be skin irritant. Always dilute with carrier oil. Do not use in bath. Not for use on children under the age of five. Not for long-term use; do not use more than ten days in a row. Do not use when pregnant or nursing. Considered moderately toxic and possibly carcinogenic. Do not use when taking anticoagulant medications; may inhibit blood clotting. Keep away from children.

Tea Tree *(Melaleuca alternifolia)*

ELEMENT: Earth

PLANT PART: Leaves, twigs

BLENDING NOTE: Middle, top

SCENT GROUP: Herbaceous

PLANT FAMILY: Myrtaceae

EXTRACTION METHOD: Steam distillation

PRECAUTIONS: Do not use when taking diabetic medications. Do not use with pregnancy or nursing. May be skin irritant. Always dilute with carrier oil. Keep away from children.

Thyme *(Thymus vulgaris)*

ELEMENT: Water, air

PLANT PART: Leaves, flowering tops

BLENDING NOTE: Middle, top

SCENT GROUP: Herbaceous

PLANT FAMILY: Lamiaceae

EXTRACTION METHOD: Steam distillation

PRECAUTIONS: May be skin irritant. Always dilute with carrier oil. Do not use in bath. Do not use with blood-clotting medications; may inhibit blood clotting. Keep away from children.

Turmeric *(Curcuma longa)*
ELEMENT: Fire
PLANT PART: Rhizome
BLENDING NOTE: Base
SCENT GROUP: Spicy
PLANT FAMILY: Zingiberaceae
EXTRACTION METHOD: Steam distillation
PRECAUTIONS: Not for use when taking diabetic medications. May be skin irritant. Always dilute with carrier oil. Do not use in bath. Do not use if pregnant or nursing. Keep away from children.

Vanilla Absolute *(Vanilla planifolia)*
ELEMENT: Water
PLANT PART: Seeds/beans
BLENDING NOTE: Base
SCENT GROUP: Spicy
PLANT FAMILY: Orchidaceae
EXTRACTION METHOD: Solvent or CO2 extraction
PRECAUTIONS: For external use only. Always dilute with a carrier oil. Keep away from children.

Vetiver *(Vetiveria zizanoides)*
ELEMENT: Earth
PLANT PART: Roots
BLENDING NOTE: Base
SCENT GROUP: Woody
PLANT FAMILY: Poaceae
EXTRACTION METHOD: Steam distillation
PRECAUTIONS: Always dilute. Keep away from children.

Violet Absolute *(Viola odorata)*
ELEMENT: Air
PLANT PART: Leaves, flowers

BLENDING NOTE: Middle
SCENT GROUP: Floral/green
PLANT FAMILY: Violacea
EXTRACTION METHOD: Solvent extraction
PRECAUTIONS: Keep away from children.

Yarrow *(Achillea millefolium)*

ELEMENT: Water
PLANT PART: Leaves, flowering tops/buds
BLENDING NOTE: Top
SCENT GROUP: Herbaceous
PLANT FAMILY: Asteraceae
EXTRACTION METHOD: Steam distillation
PRECAUTIONS: Not for use on children under
the age of five. Not for use with epilepsy. Do not
use if pregnant or nursing. Avoid with history of
endometriosis or estrogen-dependent cancer. Do
not use if taking blood-clotting medications. Do
not use if taking CYP2B6 medications or tricyclic
antidepressants. Keep away from children.

Ylang-Ylang *(Cananga odorata var. genuine)*

ELEMENT: Water
PLANT PART: Flowers
BLENDING NOTE: Base, middle
SCENT GROUP: Floral
PLANT FAMILY: Annonaceae
EXTRACTION METHOD: Steam distillation
PRECAUTIONS: Not for use on children under the
age of five. May cause skin sensitization. Always
dilute with carrier oil. Keep away from children.

Resources

Aromatherapy Education

- Aroma Apothecary Healing Arts Academy
  Shanti Dechen, founder and teacher
  www.learnaroma.com

- The School of Aromatic Studies
  Jade Shutes, founder and teacher
  https://aromaticstudies.com/about-the-school/contact/

- Floracopia
  David Crow, founder and teacher
  www.floracopia.com

Aromatherapy Supplies and Essential Oils

- Eden Botanicals
  Essential oils, supplies, carrier oils
  www.edenbotanicals.com

- Floracopia
  Essential oils, flower essences
  www.floracopia.com

- Mountain Rose Herbs
  Supplies, essential oils, herbs, carrier oils: everything you need
  www.mountainroseherbs.com

- Organic Infusions
  Essential oils, carrier oils
  www.organicinfusions.com

Bibliography

Aftel, Mandy. *Essence & Alchemy*. Layton, UT: Gibbs Smith, 2004.

Austin, Milli D. *The Healing Bath*. Rochester, Vermont: Healing Arts Press, 1997.

Beyerl, Paul. *A Compendium of Herbal Magick*. Blaine, WA: Phoenix Publishing, 2008.

Blackthorn, Amy. *Blackthorn's Botanical Magic*. Newburyport, MA: Weiser Books, 2018.

Carr-Gomm, Philip, and Stephanie Carr-Gomm. *The Druid Plant Oracle*. London: Eddison Sadd Editions Limited, 2007.

———. *The Druid Craft Tarot*. London: Eddison Sadd Editions Limited, 2004.

Cunningham, Scott. *Cunningham's Encyclopedia of Magical Herbs*. St. Paul, Minnesota: Llewellyn, 2000.

———. *Magical Aromatherapy*. Woodbury, MN: Llewellyn, 1989.

Daniels, Kooch N., and Victor. *Tarot at a Crossroads*. Atglen, PA: Schiffer, 2016.

Dechen, Shanti, *Aromatherapy Certification Level I*. Aroma Apothecary, 2011.

Decoz, Hans. "Numerology Meanings of Double-Digit Numbers." Accessed October 25, 2021. https://www.worldnumerology.com /numerology-double-digit-numbers/.

Elford, Jaymi. *Tarot Inspired Life.* Woodbury, MN: Llewellyn, 2019.

Ellena, Jean-Claude. *Perfume.* New York, NY: Arcade, 2011.

Greer, Mary K. *Archetypical Tarot: What Your Birth Card Reveals About Your Personality, Your Path, and Your Potential* (3rd edition). Weiser, 2021. (highly recommended)

———. *The Essence of Magic.* Van Nuys, CA: New Castle Publishing, 1993.

———. *Who Are You in the Tarot?* San Francisco, CA: Weiser Books, 2011.

Harrison, Karen. *The Herbal Alchemist's Handbook.* San Francisco, CA: Red Wheel/Weiser, 2011.

Hidalgo, Sharlyn. *The Healing Power of Trees.* Woodbury, MN: Llewellyn, 2010.

Jodorowsky, Alejandro, and Marianne Costa. *The Way of the Tarot.* Rochester, Vermont: Destiny Books, 2009.

Kaminski, Patricia, and Richard Katz. *Flower Essence Repertory.* Nevada City, CA: The Flower Essence Society, 2004.

Kenner, Corrine. *Tarot and Astrology.* Woodbury, MN: Llewellyn, 2011.

Kouffman Sherman, Paulette. *The Book of Sacred Baths.* Woodbury, MN: Llewellyn, 2016.

Krans, Kim. *The Wild Unknown Animal Spirit Guidebook.* The Wild Unknown, 2016.

Kusmirek, Jan. *Liquid Sunshine: Vegetable Oils For Aromatherapy.* Italy: Floramicus, 2002.

Kynes, Sandra. *Llewellyn's Complete Book of Correspondences.* Woodbury, MN: Llewellyn, 2013.

———. *Mixing Essential Oils for Magic.* Woodbury, MN: Llewellyn, 2013. (highly recommended)

Lawless, Julia. *The Complete Illustrated Guide to Aromatherapy.* London: Barnes & Noble Books, 2003.

Lembo, Margaret Ann. *The Essential Guide to Aromatherapy and Vibrational Healing.* Woodbury, MN: Llewellyn, 2016.

Miller, Light, and Bryan Miller. *Ayurveda & Aromatherapy*. Twin Lakes, WI: Lotus Press, 2012.

Millman, Dan. *The Life You Were Born to Live*. Tiburon, CA: HJ Kramer Inc. & New World Library, 1993.

Pearce, Stewart. *The Alchemy of Voice: Transform and Enrich Your Life Through the Power of Your Voice*. Scotland, UK: Findhorn Press, 2005.

Richards, Chip. *The Secret Language of Animals Oracle Deck*. Victoria, Australia: Blue Angel, 2013.

Struthers, Jane. *The Wisdom of Trees Oracle*. London: Watkins Media, 2017.

Toll, Maia. *The Illustrated Herbiary*. North Adams, MA: Storey, 2018.

Wen, Benebell. *Holistic Tarot*. Berkley, CA: North Atlantic Books, 2015.

Yronwode, Catherine. *Hoodoo Herb and Root Magic*. Forestville, CA: The Lucky Mojo Curio Company, 2016.

Zak, Victoria. *20,000 Secrets of Tea*. New York, NY: Dell, 1999.

To Write to the Author

If you wish to contact the author or would like more information about this book, please write to the author in care of Llewellyn Worldwide and we will forward your request. Both the author and the publisher appreciate hearing from you and learning of your enjoyment of this book and how it has helped you. Llewellyn Worldwide cannot guarantee that every letter written to the author can be answered, but all will be forwarded. Please write to:

Ailynn E. Halvorson

℅ Llewellyn Worldwide

2143 Wooddale Drive

Woodbury, MN 55125-2989

Please enclose a self-addressed stamped envelope for reply or $1.00 to cover costs. If outside the USA, enclose an international postal reply coupon.

Many of Llewellyn's authors have websites with additional information and resources. For more information, please visit our website:

www.llewellyn.com